FIRST STEPS IN
NEEDLEPOINT

FIRST STEPS IN
NEEDLEPOINT

Anna Pearson

Macdonald Orbis

Acknowledgments

The photographs on the following pages are by courtesy of: British Architectural Library, RIBA 88 (inset); Camera Press, London 22, 24, 27; J. & P. Coats, Edinburgh 13, 28; and Max Matheson, Photobank, London 90 (inset). The remainder of the photographs were taken by the following photographers: Jan Baldwin, Tom Belshaw, Brian Boyle, Allan Grainger, Chris Harvey, Monique Leluhandre and Jerry Tubby. The artwork was drawn by the following artists: Lindsay Blow, Andy Earl, Eugene Fleury, Jill Gordon, Suzanne Lisle, Colin Salmon, Sue Sharples and John Woodcock.

Front cover: Jan Baldwin
Half title page: Jerry Tubby
Title page: Jan Baldwin
Back cover: Jan Baldwin

A Macdonald Orbis BOOK

© Eaglemoss Publications Limited 1983, 1984

First published in Great Britain by
Orbis Publishing Limited, London 1985

Reprinted in 1987 by
Macdonald & Co (Publishers) Ltd
London & Sydney

A member of BPCC plc

This material previously appeared in the partwork *SuperStitch*

Printed in Italy

ISBN: 0 356 14325 2

Macdonald & Co (Publishers) Ltd
Greater London House
Hampstead Road
London NW1 7QX

Contents

Introduction

Needlepoint is probably enjoying greater renewed interest than any other craft. And rightly so. With new threads constantly coming onto the market to complement the traditional and tested fibres, it is extremely colourful and fun to work.

From earliest times women have used stitchery to make their homes and their dress more attractive. When designing and working needle-point you will be following a long tradition. The designs and, in particular, the materials available to us today have evolved over many centuries, and suitability for their purpose has been the guiding instinct.

Three terms used in the history of needlework can cause confusion and some clarification may be helpful.

EMBROIDERY is the art of decorating material with needlework; the background is usually left uncovered. Stitches are worked on a close-weave fabric, their length being determined by the embroiderer and the subject: they are not dependent on the number of threads in the fabric. Some of the stitches used for embroidery are the same as those used in needlepoint. Indeed, there is increasing interest in using them on canvas – see the French knots on page 53 and the chain stitch used for the ball of wool on page 51.

TAPESTRY was the forerunner of needlepoint, and needlepoint is still often incorrectly referred to as tapestry. Genuine tapestry is woven on a loom in silk and wool over a background of vertical threads. The pictorial pattern is worked in during manufacture and therefore forms an integral part of the textile.

NEEDLEPOINT is any type of work which is stitched on even-weave canvas and normally covers all the ground fabric. The earliest extant examples date from the sixteenth century. It can be pictorial, generally using tent stitch, or any type of counted work, including Florentine (Bargello) or textured stitchery. Canvas work is another acceptable term.

The fashion for decorating textiles has changed along with people's furniture and needs. During periods of uncertainty or economic difficulty sewing was plain. Only when people were more affluent and had leisure was decorative needlework pursued.

Sixteenth-century needleworkers, both professional and amateur, fashioned cushions to make the long, wooden benches that were the only form of seating more comfortable; the ambitious worked large tablecloths to cover the simple tables and cupboards. Designs were copied from the highly formal Turkey work, imported from the Near East, pieces that were much admired but very expensive.

In the seventeenth century houses became more comfortable, people had more leisure, and pattern books, illustrated with flowers and animals (both real and imaginary), were available for design reference. The influence of these books is easily seen in pieces where the scale and proportion of the animals bear no relationship to fact: obviously the needleworker had never actually seen such animals. Pictures depicting biblical scenes but with the people in contemporary costumes were popular, as too were needlepoint slips. These were individual flower or animal motifs worked on canvas and then cut out and applied to large velvet panels for bedhangings. They had a couched cord to conceal the cut canvas edges and sometimes a metal thread worked into an interlacing design on the velvet linked the appliquéd pieces.

In the eighteenth century many more families had money and education. Attractive furniture, silver and paintings became an investment. Needlework was the wife's contribution to the home. Woven fabrics for practical purposes were more generally available so the ladies of this period worked purely decorative pieces: firescreens, small pictures and other ornamental articles, all far more realistic and flowing in form than the early designs copied from Turkey work.

This trend continued into Victorian times and, with the introduction of Berlin wool-work, which used printed charts for all manner of items – foot warmers, mantle-shelf trims, needlework bags – the list of frivolous items seemed endless. Following the marked increase in the number of leisured women, the output was enormous but the quality sadly lacking.

'The arts have always travelled westward,' wrote Benjamin Franklin from London, when he was Representative of the Colonies of Pennsylvania and Massachusetts at the court of George III. As many of the new settlers in the United States were of British origin and lived on the eastern seaboard, it was natural and comparatively simple to send commissions for furniture, fabrics and needlepoint supplies via ships going to Liverpool and Southampton. It was only during the American Revolution that they took their custom to France and at the same time set up high-class workshops of their own. But it would not be unfair to say that to a great extent the renewed interest in needlepoint in the last few years has come from the States.

Today there is certainly a new enthusiasm about: an exciting willingness to combine the old and the new. Keen workers of needlepoint can obtain an ever-increasing range of fibres and ground fabrics, such as plastic canvas. Useful discontinued working aids, like perforated paper, have reappeared. Experiments are being worked with long forgotten techniques from old craft encyclopedias. Pulled thread and embroidery stitches (until recently considered only suitable for use on linen) have been tried on canvas and found to work well.

The needlepoint projects in this book range from fashion accessories, such as bags and belts, which will perk up an old outfit or be the starting point for a new one, to decorative objects like cushions, photograph frames and pictures that will look equally well in traditional or modern settings. There are also hardwearing, upholstered items, such as seats for dining chairs and dressing table stools. Or you can make and personalise a small present with the recipient's initials.

Needlepoint does not require a great deal of expensive or space-consuming equipment, and some pieces are small or simple enough to be perfect for working while travelling or while away on holiday. Even the age-old cry 'it takes so long' is not strictly true. Few of the projects have 'backgrounds' in the accepted sense of acres of tent stitch. Either they are worked in interesting, textured stitches or the designs are geometric – with all-over stitchery creating an absorbing pattern. Even more to the point, the stitching itself is really enjoyable: start with a blank canvas and see how rapidly the colours go in and patterns grow.

It is also simple enough to adapt any of the designs given in this book. Change the colours to suit your own needs and create something that is uniquely you. When the last stitch is worked you may feel a little sad – until, of course, the piece is made up, in use and receiving compliments!

You are in at a very exciting moment. Happy stitching . . .

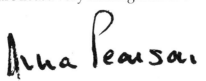

Anna Pearson, 1985

CHAPTER 1
Introducing needlepoint

*Needlepoint is the art of creating rich and beautiful embroidery
over a firm and regular framework of canvas.
Historically it is one of the oldest forms of needlework and
many of today's designs are inspired by
glorious examples from the heritage of the past.*

Needlepoint (or canvas work as it is often called) is worked on canvas or any firm fabric with evenly spaced holes. A firm, hard-wearing fabric is produced, so needlepoint is ideal for furnishings as well as smaller items, fashion accessories and pictures.

The term 'tapestry' is frequently and wrongly used when referring to needlepoint. Real tapestry is *woven* over a framework of vertical threads on a loom. In sixteenth-century Britain, when the costly woven table rugs imported from the Near East were much admired, people found that these tapestry designs could be stitched on canvas more cheaply using needlepoint.

The English tradition
Since the sixteenth century, the fashion for making particular items has changed along with people's furniture and needs – when homes had very few chairs needlewomen worked wall hangings, table carpets and cushions for their wooden benches. In the seventeenth century people sat on comfortable, upholstered chairs, and ladies stitched Bargello work covers for them: the long stitches covered the large areas quickly.

In the eighteenth century, furniture was too delicate for needlepoint which instead was used for firescreens, pictures and other small articles. This trend continued into the Victorian era and Victorian ladies stitched away at a vast range of items. Nowadays, keen workers of needlepoint have access to a dazzling array of threads and yarns. Designs are exciting and cover every taste. As well as stimulating new techniques, such as pulled thread and 'painting' on can-

Mono canvas in white (18-gauge) is a good background for bright Persian yarn.

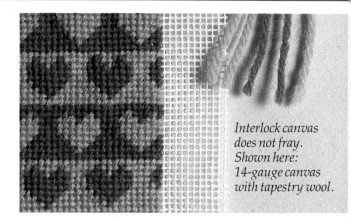

Interlock canvas does not fray. Shown here: 14-gauge canvas with tapestry wool.

Know your canvas
Most canvas is made of polished cotton or linen threads. There are two main types – mono (single thread) and Penelope (double thread). Common widths are 60cm/24in, 90cm/36in and 100cm/39in. Canvas comes in white, yellow, ecru and brown. White is best for pictorial needlepoint and for working with pale colours; ecru and brown are better for dark colours as the canvas is less likely to show between the yarn. Fine gauge canvas for petit point work often comes in yellow. When buying canvas, make sure the threads are even and shiny, not ragged or limp.

Measuring canvas mesh The measurement of canvas indicates the number of threads to 2.5cm/1in. The lower the number, the coarser the canvas: fourteen is average, and expressed as '14-gauge'. (Penelope and rug double thread canvasses are often measured in holes to 2.5cm/1in to avoid confusion over numbers of threads. Mono canvas comes in a range of 22 to 10 threads to 2.5cm/1in, and double thread canvas comes in 18 to 3 holes to 2.5cm/1in. You will soon learn to judge the most suitable canvas for your project.

Mono canvas is available in regular and interlock construction. Regular canvas has single horizontal and vertical threads woven over and under each other to form a mesh. As the threads are not bonded the canvas has a certain amount of 'give' and is the right choice for upholstery, cushions and pulled thread work.

Interlock canvas has two vertical threads woven round each horizontal one. It can be trimmed close to the finished work without fraying, so it is ideal for coasters, napkin rings, or anything with bound edges as part of the pattern. It comes in a limited number of gauges.

Penelope canvas mesh has pairs of threads – an example of a common gauge is 10/20 – ten double threads and twenty single to 2.5cm/1in. Work in a fine stitch over one thread with two strands of crewel wool, or over two threads with four.

Rug canvas has a very large mesh (usually double thread) although rugs can be worked on any canvas.

Matching canvasses and yarns When deciding which yarn to use with which canvas you can either start by choosing a canvas you enjoy working with – some people find it tiring to work with very small holes – or by choosing some particularly appealing shades of yarn. Then use the chart (far right) to guide you to a suitable combination of canvas and yarn.

vas, historical designs are being re-worked in modern colourings. People are re-discovering the pleasure of working samplers, both pictorial and geometric, to display many different stitches on one piece of work.

How to begin

When starting a piece of needlepoint make sure you are sitting comfortably in a good light.

Test the stitch and yarn on a small piece of the canvas to check that the yarn covers the canvas nicely. Thread the needle by folding the length of yarn, slipping the fold through the needle eye and pulling it through. Bring the needle through to the front of the canvas where you wish to start stitching, leaving a short length of yarn at the back. Anchor this length with your finger and work your first stitches over it to secure it. If the yarn

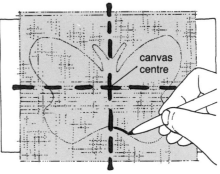

becomes twisted while you are working, let it dangle loosely from the work and it will untwist itself.

To finish off Run the needle under a few stitches on the back of the work and snip off.

Preparing canvas for working When cutting canvas allow at least 3cm/1¼in extra all round area to be stitched. Bind raw edges of the canvas with masking tape before you either mount it on a frame or begin stitching. Mark the top of canvas.

Transferring designs on to canvas If you are working needlepoint from a chart – usually given as squares each representing a stitch, begin working from the centre of the design. Find the centre of the chart (if not given) by counting squares horizontally and vertically. To find the centre of the canvas, measure and mark the centre of each edge and run two threads

across between opposite centres using running stitch. They will cross at the centre of the canvas (see diagram above).

When using a traced design, trace off the motif in fairly thick, dark lines. Position the canvas over the tracing so that the design is central or appears wherever you want it and mark the lines on to the canvas with waterproof felt-tip pen. If necessary, hold it up to the window.

Penelope canvas worked in two scales using two and four strands of crewel wool.

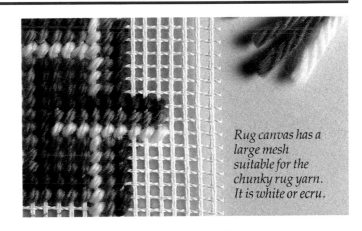

Rug canvas has a large mesh suitable for the chunky rug yarn. It is white or ecru.

Needlepoint equipment

Most pieces of needlepoint are small enough to carry around with you, and so is the necessary equipment – apart from the large floor frames.

Threads You can work needlepoint with virtually any type of thread so long as it passes easily through the canvas and covers it well.

The main types of yarn sold for needlepoint are tapestry wool, crewel wool and Persian yarn. Tapestry wool comes as an indivisible yarn similar to 4 ply knitting yarn in thickness. Crewel wool and Persian yarn are sold in thin strands that are often used in multiples for good canvas coverage. Other popular threads for needlepoint are stranded cotton, pearl cotton, metallic threads and rug yarn.

Use threads no more than 45cm/20in long to prevent them becoming weak and fluffy and so failing to cover the canvas properly.

Needles You should use a tapestry needle with a blunt point to avoid splitting the canvas threads. These come in sizes 13-24, the higher the number the finer the needle. The correct size depends on the canvas mesh and the yarn thickness – the needle

must pass through the holes comfortably without dislodging the threads and the yarn must pass through the needle eye easily without friction.

Scissors You will need a large pair for cutting canvas and small sharp embroidery scissors for the work.

Common canvasses and yarns for tent stitch

Canvas (threads to 2.5cm)	Yarn (number of strands recommended)	Size of tapestry needle
mono (22 or 24)	C (1)	24
mono (18)	C (2) P (1) T (1)	22 or 24
mono (16)	C (3) T (1)	22
mono (14 or 12)	C (3-4) P (2) T (1)	20
Penelope (10/20) over 2 threads	C (4) P (2-3)	18
over 1 thread	C (2) P (1)	24
rug (7 or 6 or 5)	P (8-9) rug (1)	16
KEY C=crewel wool, P=persian yarn, T=tapestry wool		

Choosing the right tent stitch

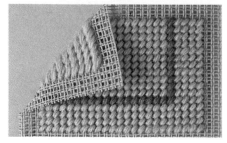 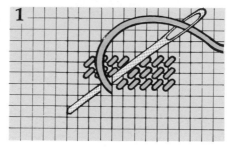 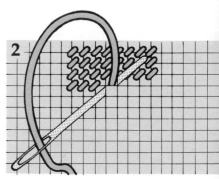

Tent stitch is the most often used needlepoint stitch. It is very versatile and is worked over only one canvas intersection making small, neat stitches on the front, longer ones on the back. It is ideal for pictorial designs, intricate patterns and smooth plain areas of background. Tent stitch forms a hard-wearing, well padded surface. There are two common forms of tent stitch – continental and diagonal.

Continental tent stitch
This is worked in horizontal rows across the canvas – from right to left and back again – and is used for outlining and small details. The back of the work is filled with long, sloping stitches (see above left).
1 Bring the needle out at the right-hand end of the row; re-insert it one hole to the right and one above, making a diagonal stitch, and bring the needle up again one hole to the left of where it first came up. Continue along the row like this.
2 On the next row (return journey), if you are holding the work, turn it upside down and work as for Step 1. Otherwise, bring the needle out in the second hole of the top line and re-insert it one hole to the left and one below to form the tent stitch. The needle comes out on the top row one hole to the right of where it first came up.

Quick and easy fragrant sachets

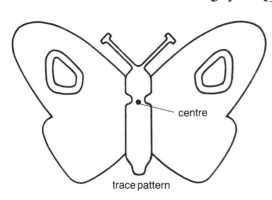

These pretty butterfly motifs can be stitched in an evening if you leave the white canvas all round the butterfly unworked. Add a canvas backing and some fragrant pot pourri or lavender – and it makes a pretty present personally stitched by you.
A fairly fine canvas is used, to prevent the pot pourri coming through. If it seems powdery, make a little muslin bag for it before inserting it into the sachet.

Two-coloured sachet
This is a simple traced butterfly in two colours framed by a double border.

You will need
One small skein each Appleton's Crewel Wool in Royal Blue 1 (821), and Sky Blue 1 (561), *or* one each of

Coral 1 (861) and Coral 3 (863)
Tapestry needle size 22
20cm/8in piece of white 18-gauge mono canvas (narrow width)
5g/¼oz dried lavender or pot pourri

Preparing the canvas
Cut two 15cm squares from the canvas, (10cm x 15cm oblongs for the smaller sachet). Bind the edges of one of the pieces with masking tape Mark the centre of the canvas and trace the butterfly outline directly on to it from the trace pattern (left), matching the centres as already described. (The centre of the trace butterfly is marked with a dot.)

Stitching the butterfly
Using the paler yarn for the body and wing markings, and the darker one for the main wing area, work in tent stitch over one thread of canvas using two strands of crewel wool. Use continental tent for the body, wing markings, and wing outline and diagonal tent to fill in. The left hand antenna is worked in stitches sloping to the left.
Remember not to leave any trailing ends of yarn which might show through. Finish them all off neatly. Next mark a square or oblong border with a pencil, 2.8 cm from the canvas edge all round and work a row of

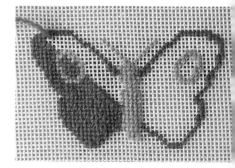

Above: Diagonal tent stitch fills in the main area of the butterfly wings.

Right: These sachets are quick to work and use both forms of tent stitch – continental and diagonal.

continental tent stitch in the paler shade. On the square sachet work a row of zigzag tent stitch border top and bottom in the dark shade as shown on page 12.

Backing and finishing
Take the other square or rectangle of canvas. Put the worked piece on top and grasp the two together so that the canvas holes align. With two strands of the darker yarn in your needle, start with a knot between the two pieces. Come through to the front and work a second row of continental tent, one thread away from the first, round three sides of the canvas. You will need to work each stitch in two movements to

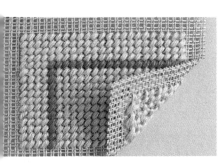

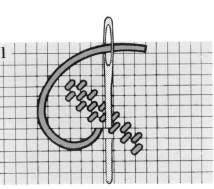

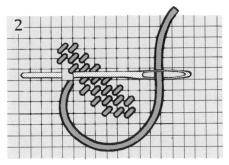

Diagonal tent stitch
This form of tent stitch is even more popular than the continental because it does not pull the canvas out of shape so much – the stitches at the back of the work being made both vertically and horizontally. It is mainly used for filling in motifs and working large areas of background.

1 Make a diagonal stitch from bottom left to top right as for continental. Then bring the needle out directly below where it goes in so that it passes under two horizontal threads, ready to make the next stitch. Your stitches will form a diagonal, downward line on the right side.

2 On the next row (return journey), the stitches are worked into the 'gaps' in the first row and the stitches on the back pass behind two vertical threads. On the front, a diagonal upward line is formed. There is no need to turn the work. The basketweave effect on the back of the canvas (see above left) means it is also sometimes known as 'basketweave tent stitch'.

make sure the border is very neat and the holes constantly aligned. At the corners, work a stitch on the end of each row to form a crossed stitch. This strengthens the corners.

Fill the sachet with the pot pourri or lavender, then work the fourth row of continental tent to close. Trim the canvas surround to within six threads of the border and pull away the loose threads to leave a pretty fringe all round.

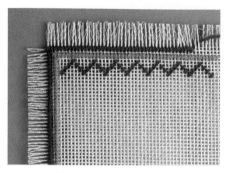

Above: After stitching the border row, fray the canvas threads to make a fringe.

Multi-coloured sachet

This highly decorative charted butterfly in misty blues, subtle corals, yellow and white can easily be worked without a frame.

You will need

1 small skein each Appleton's crewel wool in Royal Blue 1 (821) Sky Blue 1 (561), Coral 1 (861), Coral 3 (863), Bright Yellow 1 (551), and White (991)
Tapestry needle size 22
20cm/8in piece of white 18-gauge mono canvas (narrow width)
5g/¼oz dried lavender or pot pourri

Working multi-coloured sachet

The working method is very similar to the first sachet, except that the butterfly design is worked from a chart (right).

Cut two 17cm/7in squares of canvas, as this sachet is slightly larger than the two-coloured sachet.

Mark the canvas centre, and begin stitching from the centre, using two strands of yarn in the needle.

Work the stitches marked in black on the chart first – the body, antennae and main wing framework. Then work those marked in red. The repeat line on the chart shows you where to begin working the same portion of the chart on the right hand side, so that the wings are

Working chart for multi-coloured butterfly

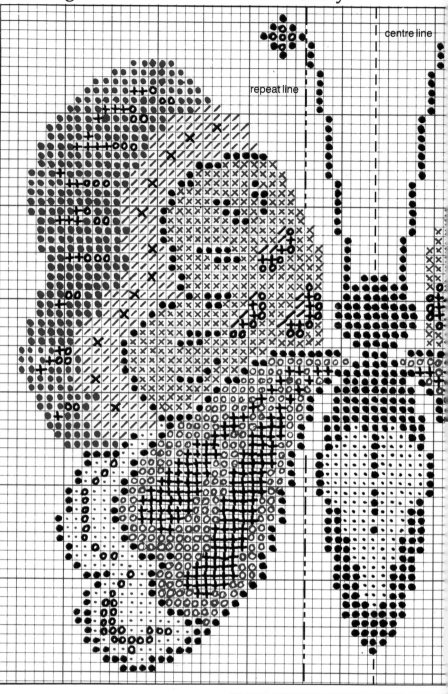

Above: Note that the chart gives the whole of the body and the left wing. To complete the right wing, work from the repeat line and reverse the pattern.

symmetrical.

Work a single border row in Royal Blue 1, positioning it about six threads away from the butterfly on each side. This row must be worked through both layers of canvas to secure the backing.

Finish off as for the two-colour sachet.

Key to chart		
yarn shade	work first	work second
821	●	●
561	·	·
861	+	
863	O	O
551	×	×
991	/	/

Diamond design to work in wool

Above: The geometric pattern is ideal for a square-shaped lampbase.

Transform a table lamp into a design feature by making an attractive needlepoint cover for the base. The diamond pattern used here is worked in trammed continental tent stitch.

Tramming – that is laying the wool along the canvas then stitching over it – gives added strength and durability to the finished article.

There are eight panels in all, separated from each other by a narrow 'stripe' of solid colour. The entire cover is worked on one rectangle of canvas. The two colour schemes used for the panels are alternated so that there are two differently coloured panels on each side of the lamp base. Either colour scheme may be varied to tone with your lampshade.

If necessary, adapt the cover size to fit a different size base. Remember, though, whether you are lengthening or widening it to work the design from the centre outwards, that is, extend it by half the amount required at each end, (or side). In this way you will always retain the proportions of the design.

You will need

Coats Anchor tapisserie wool, 4 skeins each in Peacock Blue (0168), White (0402), 3 skeins in each of Lilac (0105), Spring Green (0239), Grass Green (0246), Lilac (0576).

30cm/12in of 10-gauge Penelope (double thread) canvas, 68cm/27in wide

Wooden lampbase 8.5cm×8.5cm×22cm/3½in× 3½in×8¾in

Tapestry frame

Tapestry needle size 18

Embroidery marker

13

Preparing the canvas

Cut a piece measuring 45cm×30cm/18in×12in from the canvas. Mark the centre lengthwise and crosswise with a row of tacking stitches between a pair of double threads. Lace the canvas on to a frame (page 35). The chart shows half the length (to centre line) for a panel. Each background square represents one intersection of double threads. Using an embroidery marker, copy the half-panel design onto the canvas, placing one long edge on the vertical centre line, and the centre of panel along the horizontal centre line.
Reverse the design for the other half of the panel. Do not forget to include the single plain rows on either side of the design. Then mark out seven more panels, so that there are four on either side of the vertical centre line.

Stitching the design and making up the cover

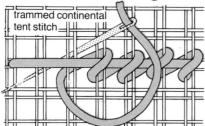

trammed continental tent stitch

Work the whole design in trammed continental tent stitch, using the chart as a colour guide. Start by stitching the centre panels, one in each of the two colour schemes. Then work outwards, alternating the colour schemes. Stitch the plain dividing rows in either Grass Green (0246) or Lilac (0576).

To work trammed continental tent stitch Referring to the diagram, make a horizontal stitch over several holes to the required length from left to right as shown, and bring the needle through directly underneath the end of the stitch. Insert the needle again, one hole to the right and one above, making one diagonal stitch. Then bring the needle through again one hole to the left of where it came up previously. Continue in this way working over the horizontal stitches in blocks, one row below the other. Note that if correctly worked, the stitches on the reverse side of the fabric should be longer than those on the right side.

Making the lampbase cover
Leaving 2.5cm/1in of canvas around the embroidery, trim away excess canvas. With right sides together, sew up the shorter sides, close to the stitching. Fold down the excess canvas at the top and bottom edges, and sew in place using herringbone stitch.
Turn the cover to the right side and slip it over the lampbase.

A quick idea for a bookmark

As an idea for using up some spare canvas and wools, why not use the design for the lamp base cover as the basis of a bookmark? On the small piece of canvas, copy out the design to a length of 20cm/8in (or whatever length of bookmark you wish to make), ensuring that you have a reasonable border of fabric all around. Work the design as given for the lampbase cover, except that the piece will be too small to put on a frame. Adapt the colour scheme to any tapestry wools you may have available.
On completion of the design, trim away the excess canvas to approximately 1cm/½in all around. Press turnings under, close to the embroidery, and catch down. For backing fabric, choose a piece of toning cotton from your scrap bag. Cut out a piece the size of the bookmark plus 1cm/½in turnings. Press under turnings, then, with wrong sides together, hand-sew in place around all edges.

Chart

top

centre

alternative colour scheme

colour guide

▨ 0168	▨ 0246	▨ 0576
☐ 0402	▨ 0239	▨ 0105

CHAPTER 2

A single stitch creates a picture

In appearance this stitch is similar to tent stitch but it is worked differently. Less yarn is carried across the back of the canvas making it economical but not so hardwearing. Use it to make a cushion or picture with this delicate orchid design.

As its name suggests, half cross stitch is worked like cross stitch, but without adding the second row of crossing stitches. Do not mix this stitch with either form of tent stitch or the work will look uneven.

Half cross stitch is sometimes worked on Penelope (double thread) canvas as well as on mono canvas. Use a frame if possible because half cross stitch can pull the canvas out of shape.

Although not as hardwearing as tent stitch, half cross stitch is always popular for pictures, fire screens and other items which do not get a lot of wear. To make a needlepoint picture, mount the finished canvas on a piece of hardboard or heavyweight card as described on page 27. This makes the next job easier for the picture framer, or for you if you are doing your own framing. It is not always a good idea to use glass in a needlepoint picture. Beware of non-reflective glass particularly as it can rot canvas, and never cover textured stitches.

The bowl of orchids design given in this chapter would look equally good as a decorative cushion, see below, or as a picture. If you choose the latter, you might like to omit the lattice border and let the picture frame take its place.

Below: A beautifully designed cushion like this fits easily into a sitting room or bedroom scheme. The blue and white border sets off the pink orchids.

Working chart for orchid design

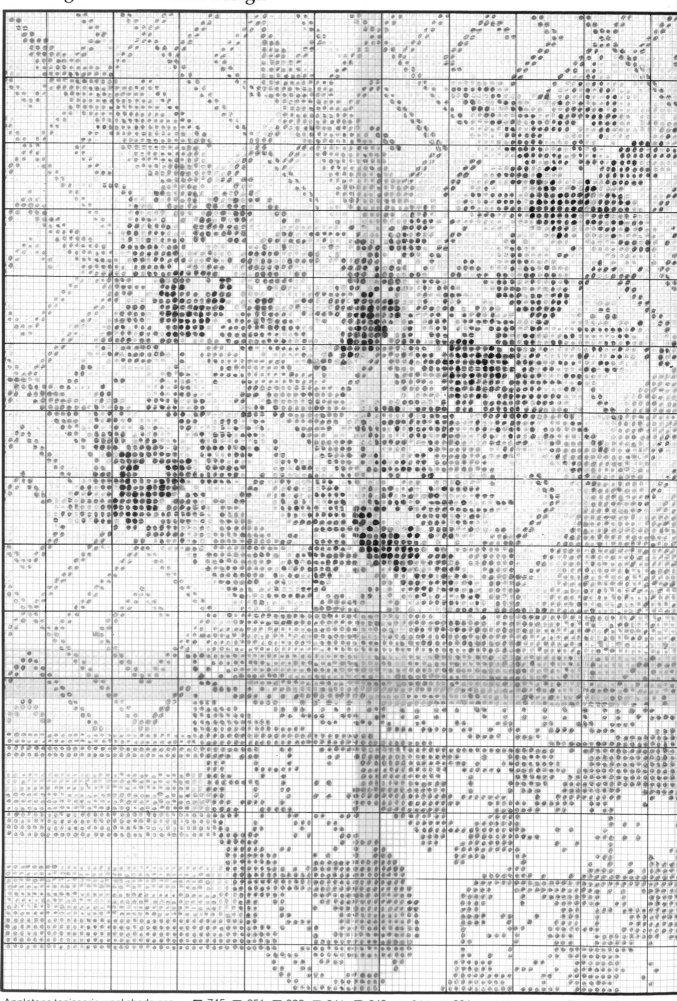

Appletons tapisserie wool shade nos   ▨ 745   ☐ 851   ☐ 992   ☐ 941   ▨ 943   ◼ 944   ▨ 204   ☐ 541   ▨ 354   ▨ 757   ☐ 471

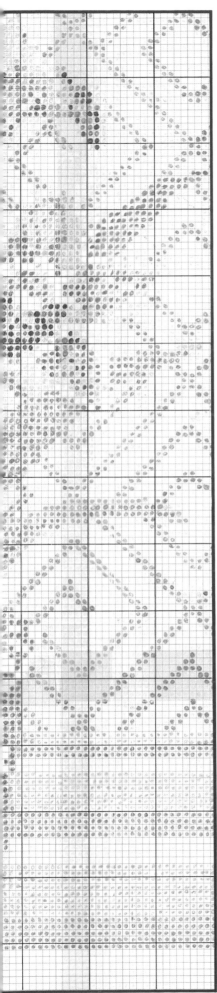

Working half cross stitch

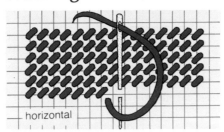

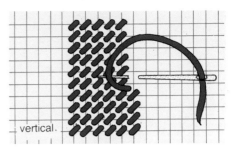

To work horizontally
Stitch from left to right as shown and turn the work at the end of each row. Straight upright stitches are formed on the back of the work.

To work vertically
To work vertical parts of a design pass the needle behind a vertical thread instead of a horizontal one.

Orchids in a Chinese bowl

This design of exotic pink orchids with a pretty blue and white lattice border is worked entirely in half cross stitch. The finished design measures 36cm/14½in square.

You will need
45cm/18in square piece of 12-gauge mono or Penelope canvas
25g/1oz hank each Appletons tapisserie wool in Bright China Blue 5 (745), Custard (851) and Off-white (992)
3 small skeins each Bright Rose Pink 1, 3 and 4 (941, 943, 944), Flame Red 4 (204), Early English Green 1 (541)
2 small skeins Grey Green 4 (354)
1 small skein each Rose Pink 7 (757) and Autumn Yellow 1 (471)
Tapestry needle size 18

Stitching the design
Bind the canvas edges with masking tape and mark the centre of the canvas. If possible, mount in a frame (see page 35).
The chart is divided into blocks of ten stitches square, so divide the

canvas in the same way using a waterproof marker to make accurate working easier. Stitch the flowers and bowl which form the main part of the design first; the background last. Use a single thickness of tapisserie wool.
Lattice border pattern Start with one of the corner squares and repeat the lattice pattern along the border beginning with a whole diamond and ending with a half diamond before the next corner square. Take care not to trail any blue yarn behind an area that will be stitched in white. When the design is complete, block and set the canvas as shown on page 23.

Making up the needlepoint
There are several ways of making up a finished needlepoint design.
Knife-edged cushion cover Take a piece of backing fabric 2.5cm/1in larger all round than the worked part of the canvas. Suitable backing fabrics are twill, rep, brocade, heavy linen, velvet and other furnishing fabrics.
With right sides together machine the canvas and backing along three and a half sides, leaving an opening along the lower edge of the cushion. Turn to right side, insert a cushion pad slightly larger than the cover and hand stitch the opening.
Cushion with border To make a larger cushion, buy a ready-made cushion cover of the required size and mount the needlepoint on it. Trim the edges to 1cm/½in and turn under. Pin the canvas centrally in place and slipstitch firmly all round the edge.

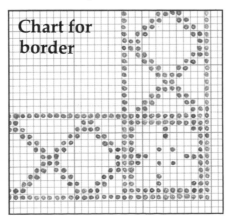

Chart for border

Note: On both charts each dot represents one half cross stitch

CHAPTER 3

Rug yarns and canvas for large-scale projects

Much historical needlepoint consisted of working rugs in imitation of Oriental woven designs. You can still do this today – in fact all kinds of designs make beautiful rugs. This colourful cow design is fun to work and looks good in a child's room.

Needlepoint rugs can be both lovely to look at and practical providing you choose yarn and stitches carefully. Rugs tend to be too ambitious a project for needlepoint beginners, so perfect your stitches and techniques before attempting one.

Planning a needlepoint rug

Take plenty of time to decide on the size, shape and colour of your rug – once begun, it may take you some time to complete and you must be sure it suits your requirements exactly.

Now decide whether to make it all in one piece, or in smaller squares which you can join together when complete. A rug worked in one piece, or as a central panel with borders added will wear far better than a rug consisting of several joined panels. However, a large, single piece of canvas is less convenient to work on than several smaller pieces.

Choosing materials and stitches

In theory, you can stitch a rug on any gauge of canvas from very fine to the coarse rug canvas – finer canvasses will take longer! Check the different widths in which your chosen canvas is available – you could save yourself some unnecessary joining of pieces. If you plan a separate border or a design of different squares, all the canvas for the rug must be cut from the same roll. Adjoining squares with a discrepancy of even one canvas thread will not match up satisfactorily.

Suit the yarn to the canvas in the usual way, making sure canvas coverage is as good as it can be for maximum wear, whether you are working in crewel, persian, tapestry, thrums (carpet manufacturers' off-

cuts), or rug wool. Of course, the finer the yarn and canvas, the longer it will take you to cover a given area. Chunky four or six-ply rug wool makes lovely stitched rugs – use a heavy, blunt rug needle. It is sold in skeins and can be used for cross or half cross stitches, straight gobelin stitch and gobelin filling stitch.

Other suitable stitches for the finer yarns which are available are basket-weave tent stitch and all types of cross stitch including the decorative crossed corners.

Florentine patterns make dramatic rugs which are quick to make. Always choose designs with stitches that are not too long as these can snag when the rug is in use.

For a rug with a fluffy, raised pile, use one of the looped or cut pile stitches.

If the design requires a number of skeins of yarn in one colour, these must come from the same dye lot to ensure colour matching.

Working a needlepoint rug

It is easier, but not essential, to work heavier rugs in a frame. If possible, work on a frame with a floor stand and mount the canvas with the selvedges at the sides. Allow at least 4cm/1½in of canvas outside the stitching on each piece. Transfer the design to the canvas in the normal way, unless you are working from a chart. Start stitching at one end with the unworked canvas away from you. As far as possible, work in horizontal rows but, obviously, work separate motifs as they appear in the design. Block and set the finished work as described on page 23.

Joining the rug sections

If your rug is in several square, or

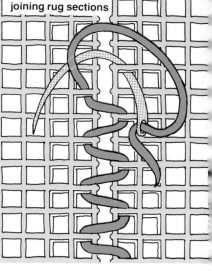

joining rug sections

rectangular sections, or has an added border, join the worked squares together by hand, using blind stitch and invisible thread, or, for very heavy pieces, carpet or button thread. Lay the canvas right side up on a table so that the pieces are supported. Press unworked canvas to the back on both edges to be joined and lay them together so that they just meet. Using a curved needle pick up one thread of large gauge canvas or two threads of 10-gauge canvas or finer canvas on the folded edge of one of the pieces. Now pick up a corresponding number of threads on the folded edge of the other piece, exactly opposite the point where the needle emerged from the last stitch. Continue in this way until all pieces and borders are joined.

If you are joining larger pieces of canvas for all-over designs, overlap the edges 4cm/1½in and tack with strong thread. Work through double canvas when stitching the design.

Finishing off the rug

It is important to turn over the edges and mitre the corners of the rug neatly.

If you're adding a fringe to the ends of the rug, leave one or two rows of canvas showing on the right side and mitre canvas and stitch edges as described below.

Trim unworked canvas equally all round to about 3cm/1¼in and fold the four corners diagonally towards the centre on the back.

Press the fold firmly to keep it flat.

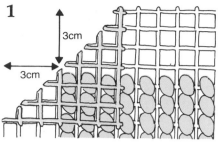

2 Fold one straight edge over to the centre and press well. Fold and press the other edge and stitch along each diagonal seam.

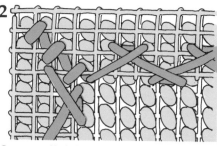

Secure all the edges on the back with herringbone stitch. This is all the finishing that some rugs will need unless a fringe is required.

Cows in a field rug

A softly twisted rug yarn makes this chunky rug a welcome addition to a playroom. It measures 69cm × 102cm/27in × 40in. Work the rug on double thread (Smyrna) rug canvas. Use cross stitch for a hard wearing rug or half cross stitch as shown here to cut down on time and cost.

You will need

15m/1¼yd DMC rug canvas (width 69cm/27in, 5 double threads to 2.5cm/1in)
Rug needle
DMC Soudan wool, to work in half cross stitch:
5 skeins in 7344, 3 skeins in 7469, 2 skeins each in 7314, 7428, WHITE, 7184 and 7341, 1 skein each in 7435, 7164, 7351, 7133, 7310 and 7445
For fringe: 1 skein each in 7314 and 7344 (optional)
To work in full cross stitch, buy 9 extra skeins in 7344, 3 in 7469, 4 each in 7314, 7428, WHITE, 7184 and 7341, and 1 in 7351

Working the rug

Stitch the design from the chart – one square equals one half cross stitch. Use a single thickness of Soudan wool, in 45cm/18in lengths. To complete, fold back the two short ends of the rug leaving two double rows of canvas showing and secure with herringbone stitch. Add a sky colour fringe at the top and a grass colour at the bottom.
Finally, overcast the two long edges.

Right: An appealing rug in a lovely combination of colours – try adapting other simple children's pictures, too.

Chart for rug

1 square = 1 half cross stitch

7184 7469 7445 7133 7344 7164 7351 7314 7428 7341 7435 7310 white

Rug and carpet fringes for trimming

You may wish to add a decorative fringe to the ends of your rug.

In general, it is best to use the same yarn as that used for stitching the rug, but for Persian-type designs, a traditional cotton fringe is often knotted on to either end to look like the warp threads of a real woven rug. You'll need a crochet hook and a pair of sharp scissors for trimming the finished fringe. If possible, the strands should share holes with the outside row of needlepoint stitches to avoid having a row of bare threads showing.

Cutting the fringe

Depending on the yarn, 15cm/6in strands will give you a fringe of about 5cm/2in. As a rough guide, double the depth of fringe required and add 5cm/2in for the knot. Cut even strands by winding yarn round a piece of cardboard the depth of the fringe plus 2.5cm/1in and cutting through the yarn along one side.

Simple knotted fringe

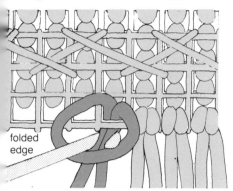

folded edge

With the back of the rug upwards, insert crochet hook through edge hole close to stitching. Catch the cut length (or lengths) of yarn in the centre, and pull a loop through to the back.

Pass the loose ends through this loop and pull tight.

A smoother effect is obtained by working with rug front uppermost.

Plaited heading with knots

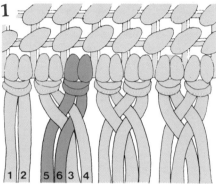

1 2   5 6 3 4

This adds decoration to a plain fringe and looks attractive worked in rug yarn.

1 Plait the ends in groups of four. Leave first pair of strands (1/2) loose.

Pass strand 5 over strand 4, strand 3 over strand 5 and strand 6 under strand 4 and over strand 3. Repeat with the next four strands.

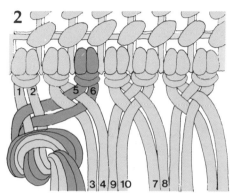

1 2   5 6   3 4 9 10   7 8

2 Now hold strands 1 and 2 with strands 5 and 6 and knot them. Continue plaiting and knotting along the fringe making sure the knots are tied at exactly the same level as the first one.

Overhand knot fringe

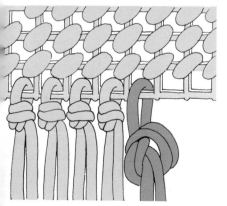

To make more of a feature of the knots, thread the length (or lengths) of yarn through the hole. Hold the back and front ends together and tie tightly in an ordinary overhand knot, close up to the edge of the canvas.

Alternating knots fringe

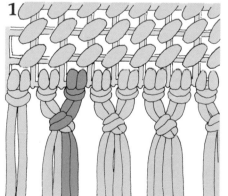

A pretty fringe with a diamond pattern at the top which requires a little extra yarn. It can be worked in groups of four on a simple knotted fringe or under a plaited heading.

1 Knot pairs of strands together all the way across the fringe to form groups of four, having all the knots level about 1cm/½in away from the top of the fringe.

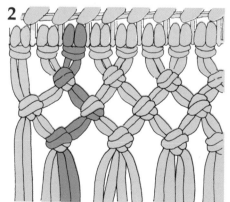

2 Now work a second row of knots, about 1cm/½in below the first, taking two strands from one group and two strands from the next. Work as many rows of knots as you like before trimming the fringe evenly, but the loose fringe should be left longer than the knotted band.

CHAPTER 4

Variations in straight stitch create texture and pattern

Straight stitches in needlepoint are easy to work and cover the canvas quickly. Exciting patterns and textures are made simple and show the colours of the yarn to best advantage, so enjoy the freedom of straight stitches and embroider a colourful picture in several stitch variations.

There are several different types of straight stitches for use on canvas. Many different textures and effects can be created by varying the length and direction of the stitches.

Straight stitch techniques

Straight stitches are ideal for pictorial needlepoint and form clean-edged areas of colour. Subtle, shaded effects are also possible and often found in Florentine stitchery – one of the most well-known forms of straight stitch work.

Straight stitches are often worked over several canvas threads at a time. This is why you can finish a piece of straight stitch work comparatively fast. It is important to get canvas coverage right, and you will probably find you need a thicker thread than for tent stitch on the same gauge of canvas. (Use the guide given for tent stitch on page 9, and add an extra strand to the recommended thread thickness.)

Some types of straight stitch are not very hard-wearing. If stitches are very long, they can become loose and fluffy with too much wear, so they are best confined to pictures, wall-hangings and the like.

Working methods

You can work straight stitches horizontally, vertically, in neat rows geometric patterns or at random – in fact, almost any way you like. Experiment on small pieces of spare canvas when you are testing for good canvas coverage. By changing the direction of stitches on a piece of work, you can emphasize different parts of a design. The light will catch them in a different way.

Where possible, bring the needle up in an empty hole, and push it down through a filled one. The yarn will pass more easily through the canvas and will not bring up fluffy strands of other colour yarns to spoil the look of the finished work.

In general, straight stitches do not distort the canvas nearly as much as tent and other diagonal stitches. You will often find that you can work effectively without a frame, particularly on smaller pieces of canvas. Mono canvas is the most suitable for this type of work.

Texture and pattern

The house picture (left) is an ideal example of how you can use straight needlepoint stitches to create different textural effects. All the stitches in the picture lie vertically yet, by varying their length and the way they are worked together, you can portray sky, roofs, trees, bricks and paving. Try out different stitches on spare canvas. Find out which stitch is most effective for each part of the picture you are working. Here, the walls of the house are worked in blocks of straight stitches positioned to look like bricks. The sky, in gently undulating graduated straight stitch, is a good foil for the foreground detail. Notice the clever tile effect on the red roof, and how the same stitches, reversed, are used for the paving stones on the path. A diagonal line pattern makes a perfect front door. The ends of the stitches are used to 'draw' the lines in the picture.

*Left: This colourful house picture incorporates several different textures.
Right: Take a closer look at the patterns. From top left to bottom right: sky, roof, bricks, tree, garden path, front door.*

Four well-known straight stitches

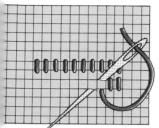 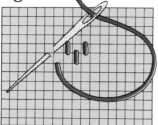 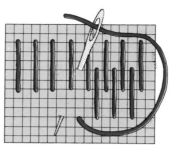 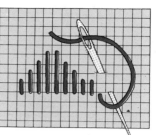

Straight gobelin stitch

This simple stitch resembles those on the famous Gobelin tapestries. The stitches are worked to a uniform length in horizontal rows, and are good for borders and for large areas.

Work over two to five canvas threads, from left to right and back again. Bring the needle out on the left and reinsert it two threads above. Bring it out again in the next hole to the right of where it first came up.

Brick stitch

This stitch is normally worked over two or four canvas threads. The interlocking rows form an all-over texture that is a useful filling. When changing colours the slight overlap between the rows creates a pleasing shaded effect. Work alternate up-and-down stitches as shown to make a zigzag row. The next row is worked directly underneath, so that the stitches lie end to end, and each one shares a canvas hole with the one in the row above.

Gobelin filling stitch

A close relation of brick stitch, gobelin filling stitch gives a slightly different effect, being worked over six threads or more (but it must be an even number). Work each row in vertical straight stitches, leaving an empty row between each stitch. On the next row, work stitches in the empty rows, three threads lower than those in the first row. For a straight edge, work stitches over three threads to fill the gaps left by the last full row.

Graduated straight stitch

By working straight stitches of varying length, you can fill almost any shape satisfactorily. Geometric patterns can be interpreted very well in this stitch, and many interesting textures can be created. Try aligning one end of all the stitches to create a 'wave' effect (as shown above), or working an area of horizontal stitches. The working method is the same as for straight gobelin stitch, except for the length of the stitches.

Blocking and setting needlepoint

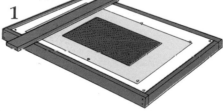 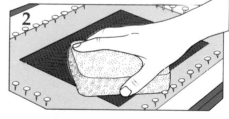

All needlepoint benefits from being blocked when completed. The process ensures that all the canvas threads end up straight, with any patterns or pictures the right shape and not distorted in any way. It also gives a smooth texture to the stitchery.

Dampening the canvas and allowing it to dry will reset the canvas threads correctly. Check that you have not missed any stitches – hold it up to the light and fill in gaps.

1 Take a piece of wooden board larger than the piece of work, which will take tacks. Fix a piece of white sheet over this and nail the canvas on to it, right side upwards so as not to flatten any raised-texture stitches. Use a steel ruler to get the edges absolutely straight.

Nail down two opposite sides and then the other two sides using rust-proof tacks at about 2cm/¾in intervals. Stretch the work into shape as you go. If necessary, use a tracing of the design placed over the worked canvas to get it exactly straight.

2 Dampen the canvas by dabbing with a wet sponge until it is really wet. Do not scrub, but use a blotting motion. You should not dampen any work incorporating silk threads, and some of the very dark shades of crewel wool and tapestry wool are not guaranteed colour-fast, so be very careful with these where they adjoin pale colours. Be sure that any markers or paints used on canvas are colour-fast before you dampen it. Leave it flat to dry naturally and completely. This will take at least 48 hours.

23

Colourful cushions using simple straight stitches

A splash of colour, using a range of colourful yarns, is created using the simple straight gobelin stitch to create a pair of cushions. You can choose the same colour tints as shown here, or interpret the patterns in your own blend of colours to suit the furnishings of your room. They could also look effective using the entire range of one colour.

The striped cushion

The colours are gently graded in narrow bands across the cushion starting with the greens, through the blues to the reds.

You will need

50cm×55cm/20in×22in piece of 12-gauge mono canvas
50cm×55cm/20in×22in piece of backing fabric – dark green or blue is best
45cm×50cm/18in×20in cushion pad

2 skeins Paterna Persian yarn in each of the following colours:
dark green, mid green, pale green, light blue, blue/green, dark blue/green, dark blue, mauve, pale mauve, pale violet, mid violet, dark violet, reddish pink, deep dusty pink, pale dusty pink, light red, aubergine, deep reddish brown.
Tapestry needle size 20
Finished size of cushion about 45cm×50cm/18in×20in.

Stitching the design

As straight gobelin stitch does not pull and distort the canvas it is not essential to mount it on a frame although you may find it easier to work using one.
Bind the edges of the canvas with masking tape to stop them fraying.
Mark the outline of the finished cushion size centrally on the canvas

Above: The range of tones used in the square and rectangular cushions creates a rich effect. If you are planning your own colour scheme it is worth experimenting on paper with coloured pencils first to achieve a harmonious balance of colour.

with a pencil or waterproof marker. The stitch is worked over seven threads, so the width of the cushion must be 252 threads. The depth should measure 45cm/18in but the number of threads is not critical. This will leave a 2.5cm/1in border all round for making up.
Following the chart and colour key opposite, work the canvas within the pencil-marked area in straight gobelin stitch as shown in the diagram. Each of the numbered divisions on the chart represents two rows (14 threads of the canvas) worked in one colour. There are

eighteen different colours of yarn worked on a total of 36 rows, two in each colour. Each stitch is over seven threads of canvas and using at least three strands of wool in the needle to give a good coverage. Do not pull the stitches too tight as you work or they will not lie flat on the canvas.

Making up the cushion
With the right side of the needlepoint and backing fabric together, machine or hand stitch all round three sides, stitching as close to the edge of the gobelin embroidery as possible (about 2.5cm/1in seam allowance). Trim seams to 1cm/½in, cutting across each corner diagonally to reduce bulk.
Turn to the right side and insert the cushion pad. Oversew the fourth side by hand to close the remaining seam. If you wish to remove the cover for cleaning, simply unpick this seam to remove the pad.

The checked cushion
Almost all the same colours from the striped cushion are used on the checked version but a different effect

is achieved by placing them in diagonal blocks of colour.

You will need
55cm×55cm/22in×22in piece of 12-gauge mono canvas
55cm×55cm/22in×22in piece of backing fabric – dark green or blue is best
45cm×50cm/18in×20in cushion pad
3 skeins Paterna Persian yarn in each of the following colours: dark green, mid green, pale green, blue/green, dark blue/green, dark blue, mauve, pale mauve, pale violet, mid violet, reddish pink, deep dusty pink, pale dusty pink, light red, aubergine, deep reddish brown.
Tapestry needle size 20
Finished size of cushion about 45cm×50cm/18in×20in.

Stitching the design
As with the striped cushion, it is not essential to mount the canvas on a frame but bind the edges with masking tape to prevent fraying. Mark the outline of the finished cushion size centrally on the canvas. Each block is made up of four sets of stitches worked over

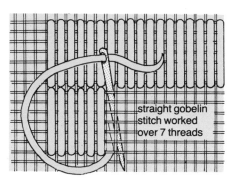

straight gobelin stitch worked over 7 threads

seven threads so again the width of the cushion is 252 threads. The depth of each block is 28 stitches so the total depth of the cushion is 224 threads. There is a 2.5cm/1in seam allowance all round.
Starting at the top left-hand corner work the first square in straight gobelin stitch so that it extends 28 stitches down the canvas and four rows of seven threads across the canvas.
Follow the chart above for the arrangement of the different colours or work your own colour scheme if you prefer.

Making up the cushion
Assemble the cushion in the same way as for the striped cushion.

Chart for striped cushion

| 1 | 2 | 3 | 4 | 5 | 6 | 7 | 8 | 9 | 10 | 11 | 12 | 13 | 14 | 15 | 16 | 17 | 18 |

Chart for checked cushion

1	2	3	5	6	7	8	9	10
2	3	5	6	7	8	9	10	11
3	5	6	7	8	9	10	11	13
5	6	7	8	9	10	11	13	14
6	7	8	9	10	11	13	14	15
7	8	9	10	11	13	14	15	16
8	9	10	11	13	14	15	16	17
9	10	11	13	14	15	16	17	18

1 dark green	**5** blue/green	**9** pale mauve	**13** reddish pink	**17** aubergine
2 mid green	**6** dark blue/green	**10** pale violet	**14** deep dusty pink	**18** deep reddish brown
3 pale green	**7** dark blue	**11** mid violet	**15** pale dusty pink	
4 light blue	**8** mauve	**12** dark violet	**16** light red	

Angel nursery picture

Any child would love to be watched over by this merry little angel floating in a starry sky. The finished picture measures 22cm×21.5cm/8¾in×8½in and is worked in straight stitches on an easy-to-work 14-gauge canvas. All the stitches lie in one direction. The canvas can be held – a frame is not essential.

You will need
1 piece white mono canvas, 14 threads to 2.5cm/1in, measuring 32cm/12½in square

Coats Anchor tapisserie wool:
 2 skeins 0132, 1 skein each 0894, 0573, 0738, 0740, 0295, 0732
Tapestry needle size 18
Waterproof marker, masking tape

Preparing the canvas
Bind the raw edges of the canvas with masking tape, and mark the

centre. Place the canvas centrally over the trace pattern and mark on the design lines using a waterproof marker.

If you find it hard to see the design through the canvas, trace off the picture in thick, black lines and hold the canvas up to the window when transferring the lines on to it.

Trace pattern for angel

Stitch key

A gobelin filling stitch over 8 threads

B gobelin filling stitch over 6 threads

C straight gobelin stitch over 2 threads

D graduated straight stitch

E small straight stitches

F double cross stitches

Colour key

☐ hair and stars 0295

☐ face and hands 0740

▨ clouds 0738

☐ wings 0732

▨ sky and eyes 0132

☐ top part of robe 0894

▨ lower part of robe 0894, 0573, 0732

▨ mouth and shoes 0573

Stitching the picture

Following the colour and stitch key, work the angel design in different straight stitches. Try as far as possible to cover the marked outlines. The clouds, angel's hair, face and wings are worked in graduated straight stitch, with the stitches ending along the pattern lines. Work the design on the angel's robe in straight gobelin stitch with the stitches in pairs worked over two threads in diagonal rows. Use the deep pink as the main colour, with little 'checks' in pale pink and off-white. Work tiny straight stitches for eyes, mouth, hands and feet. Finally, add some gold stars – each one a double cross stitch. To work, make a big upright cross stitch on the blue sky, and a smaller one on top at 45° to it.

Finishing off

Make sure you have covered the whole of the picture area with stitches and fill in any missed ones. Block the canvas as described on page 23, using a tracing of the design given here to make sure it is the correct shape.

Mounting the picture

You can have the work mounted and framed professionally. It is also simple to mount needlepoint yourself, on hardboard. If the picture is to be framed, use a piece of hardboard which allows a margin all round for the frame overlap. Otherwise, take a piece measuring the same as the stitched area, and stretch the canvas over it. Secure the canvas all along the cut edges of the hardboard with pins or tacks. Pin two opposite edges, then fold the other two sides of the canvas over, and secure those.

When all four sides have been pinned and the picture looks straight, lace the opposite edges tightly across the back with fine string or strong thread. Cover with a piece of backing fabric, the edges turned in neatly and slip-stitched to the needlepoint. Screw two ring-hooks into the board (through the fabric) and tie string between for hanging.

Below: Be sure to keep the ends of whole blue background stitches (over the full eight threads) in even horizontal rows.

Bright and cheerful embroidered bag

Above: This bag is quick to work and makes a colourful accessory.

Bright rayon yarn makes an attractive thread for needlepoint. The embroidery is worked on to double thread canvas which makes the bag stronger.

You will need

2 pieces 35cm/14in square double thread canvas 11/12 holes per 2.5cm/1in
3–4 skeins 100% rayon yarn (raffia substitute) in burgundy, 3 skeins in mid-blue, 2 skeins in turquoise and 1 skein each of dark pink, golden yellow, yellow, dark green and jade green
1 large tapestry needle

6 small beads (optional)
40cm/16in lining fabric
Matching sewing thread

Working the embroidery

Enlarge the graph pattern for the bag – each square is 2.5cm/1in. Cut out two bag shape pieces in canvas adding 2cm/¾in all round for seams. Transfer the flower pattern on to the canvas using a soft pencil.

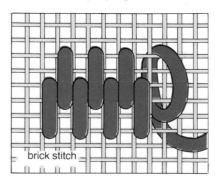

brick stitch

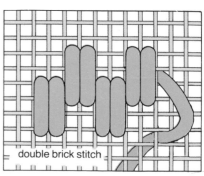

double brick stitch

28

Graph for embroidered bag

1 square = 2.5cm

Using the rayon yarn, work the flowers, leaves and stems in satin stitch following the colours in the photograph. Stitch each petal separately across the width. Next work the background in burgundy in brick stitch over four threads.

Work the top strip of the bag design in double brick stitch over four threads. If desired, sew three small beads to the centre of each flower.

Press the two bag halves lightly using a damp cloth on the wrong side. Turn the seam allowance on the top edge to the wrong side and press.

Place the two bag halves, right sides facing, and stitch together leaving the top edge open. Trim the seam allowance to 1cm/½in.

Lining the bag

To line the bag, cut two halves in lining fabric and adding 1cm/½in seam allowance all round. Place the pieces of lining right sides facing and sew together leaving top edge open. Press the seam allowance to the wrong side along the top edges.

Turn the embroidered bag through to the right side and insert the lining so that the wrong sides are facing. Neatly hand sew the lining to the bag along top edges.

Making the strap

To make a strap with a finished length of 2m/80in, cut six 6m/6½yd lengths of mid-blue rayon and four in turquoise.

Tie all the ends together 10cm/4in from each end and then twist them together until they form a cord about 2m/80in long.

Stitch the cord along the edge of the bag, starting in the centre of the lower edge and leaving the untwisted end as a tassel. Neatly stitch by hand up one side of the bag. Leave a length free for the shoulder strap and then stitch the cord down the other side of the bag, leaving the other untwisted end as a tassel.

CHAPTER 5
Chunky cross stitches

*The cross stitch family is one of the largest in needlepoint.
All the stitches are sturdy and suitable
for working handsome geometric designs on useful items
that need to be strong and hardwearing, such
as the glasses case and clutch bag in this chapter.*

Cross stitches can be worked on mono or Penelope canvas. Some form square patterns, some diamonds and some rectangles. This geometric character makes them simple to master – from the basic cross stitch over two canvas threads, to the larger eye-catching triple cross stitch.

Tent stitch is a good accompaniment to some cross stitch variations – filling in spaces between them.

Basic know-how

The general rule that applies to the whole cross stitch family is that the last part of the stitch worked should always lie in the same direction. When a stitch incorporates an upright cross stitch, it is always the horizontal thread that is placed last. It is well worth trying out all the variations on spare canvas before tackling any projects.

Regular cross stitch

Cross stitch can be worked either horizontally or vertically, in single complete stitches, or in two-stage rows of half cross stitches. To be sure of always having the crossing stitches sloping in the same direction, work along a row in half cross stitches, and then back again to complete the crosses. For small motifs such as initials, you will find it easier to work in complete stitches.

Horizontal cross stitch

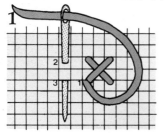 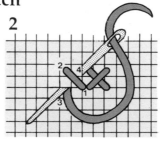

Working from right to left, over two threads:
1 Bring the needle out at (1) and re-insert at top left (2) to come out at bottom left (3).

2 Re-insert it at top right (4) to complete the stitch, and bring it out again at bottom left, ready to work another stitch.

Oblong cross stitch

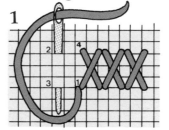 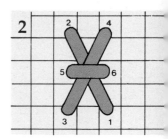

1 To work it over two threads, make an elongated cross stitch over four horizontal threads and two vertical threads.

2 Create a more decorative effect by adding a small catching stitch across the centre, over two threads as shown.

Vertical cross stitch

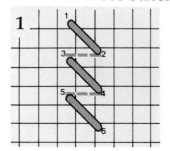 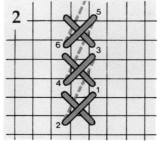

Working in two-stage rows of half stitches:
1 Make a diagonal stitch from top left (1) to bottom right (2) over the required number of threads (in this case, two). Bring the needle out at bottom left (3) and continue making downward diagonal stitches to bottom of row.

2 Beginning at top right of bottom stitch (1), make a diagonal stitch to bottom left (2), crossing the first one, and bring the needle out at top right of the stitch above (3). Continue to the end of the row. This makes long crossing stitches on the back of the work.

Crossed corners

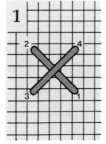

This is sometimes known as rice stitch, and is a useful hardwearing filling or border stitch. It looks striking when the corner stitches are worked in a contrasting, sometimes finer, yarn.
1 Work a large cross stitch over four threads.
2 Work four small

diagonal stitches over the corners as shown.
Always bring the needle up in the hole opposite to where it last went in.
3 When the corner stitches are in a contrasting yarn, work a row of large cross stitches first, and then 'cross the corners' using the new yarn.

Double cross stitch

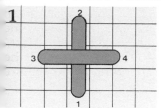

This pretty stitch is often worked in two shades.
1 Work an upright cross stitch over four canvas threads.

2 Next work a small diagonal cross stitch over two threads on top of it, forming a diamond pattern. Remember to keep the last stitches sloping the same way.

Below: Two needlepoint gifts to make. The bag and glasses case are worked in a combination of blue and deep rose pink. They would look just as good in black with gold thread.

Triple cross stitch

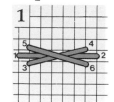

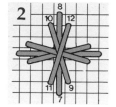

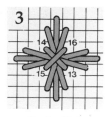

This exciting stitch gives the effect of raised star shapes. Fill the gaps with cross or tent stitches.
1 Make a horizontal stitch over eight threads and work an oblong cross stitch on top (over six vertical threads and two horizontals).

2 Make a vertical stitch over eight threads. Now work another oblong cross stitch on top of this, (over six horizontal threads and two verticals).
3 Finish with a central regular cross stitch (two threads) over all these stitches.

Delightful small gifts in cross stitch variations

The geometric shapes of the cross stitch family make them suitable for working all kinds of simple items based on square and rectangular shapes. To start you off, here are patterns for two quick-to-make gifts – a glasses case and a clutch bag with a needlepoint flap.

The raised texture of the cross stitches gives a strong as well as pretty finish. Notice how the stitches complement the designs. Oblong cross stitch in the glasses case is combined with crossed corners, which sets up an unusual rhythm. The bag flap features two diamond shaped stitches to echo its V-shape.

Clutch bag

This beautiful clutch bag has a richly embroidered needlepoint flap, divided into vertical panels bordered by

cross stitch. It includes the decorative triple cross stitch in two shades of pink. The stitched flap extends just over the top of the bag, but if you wish, you can continue the stitchery right down the back of the bag and up the front, too.

You will need

25cm/¼yd piece of 14-gauge mono canvas (narrow width)
3 small skeins each Appleton's crewel wool in Bright China Blue 7 (747), Bright Rose Pink 8 (948) and Bright Rose Pink 5 (945)
Tapestry needle size 20
Waterproof marker, masking tape

Below: The chart shows half of the symmetrical design for the clutch bag flap. Just work the other half of the design in reverse to complete the flap.

For making up

50cm/½yd toning fabric (any width)
25cm×50cm/9¾in×19¾in piece buckram (optional)
Large press stud fastening

Working the flap

Bind the canvas and mark the flap outline on to it by counting threads. The stitched area is 136 threads wide and 84 threads deep at the point.
Work very carefully from the chart by counting threads. Each of the five vertical panels covers 24 vertical threads, and the lines of cross stitches between them are worked over two threads. Begin at the centre and work outwards.
After completing the charted design, work one row of tent stitch in blue round the edge of the whole

Glasses case

The glasses case, stitched in an all over pattern, is a smaller project. Each diagonal row of crossed corners is worked in a different shade of pink or burgundy in a random order so it is marvellous for using up oddments of leftover yarn. Only one side of the case is embroidered.

You will need

20cm/¼yd piece of 18-gauge mono canvas (narrow width)
3 small skeins Appleton's crewel wool in Bright China Blue 7 (747)
Skeins of yarn in 5 other shades of pink and burgundy such as Appleton's Bright Rose Pink 1, 3, 4, 6 and 8 (941, 943, 944, 946, 948) or Paterna Persian yarn 850 and 855
Tapestry needle size 20
Waterproof marker and masking tape.

For making up

25cm/¼yd toning fabric (any width)
40cm/16in square buckram
Fabric adhesive

Working the glasses case

Cut the canvas to 20cm×27cm/7¾in ×10¾in and bind edges with masking tape. Mark canvas centre, and mark the outline of the case with a waterproof marker by counting the threads. (The length covers 100

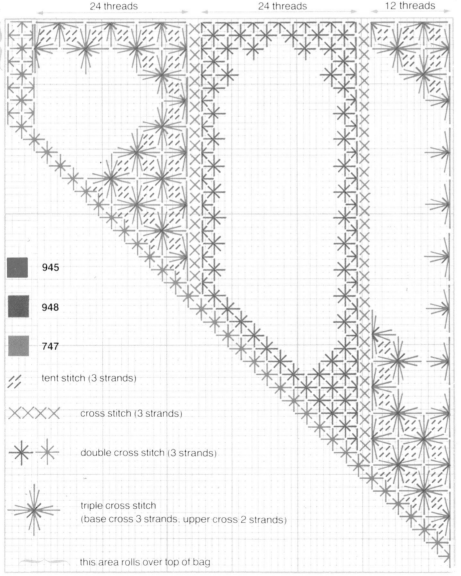

24 threads   24 threads   12 threads

945

948

747

tent stitch (3 strands)

cross stitch (3 strands)

double cross stitch (3 strands)

triple cross stitch
(base cross 3 strands, upper cross 2 strands)

this area rolls over top of bag

worked area to make the turnings neat. Work an extra row across the back edge.

Making up the bag
You can either have the bag made up professionally, or assemble the simple envelope shape yourself. Cut a paper pattern with measurements as shown. Draw sides AB, CD, and AC. Next draw EF down the centre. Join FB and FD to make the V-shaped flap. Fold fabric in half lengthwise and cut out the bag piece (double). Block needlepoint, or press carefully, pulling it to the correct shape. Trim canvas border to 1cm/½in and turn under canvas on long back edge of flap, tacking it in place. Place wrong side of needlepoint on right side of one bag piece with edges flush. Tack in place, and stitch all round close to needlepoint

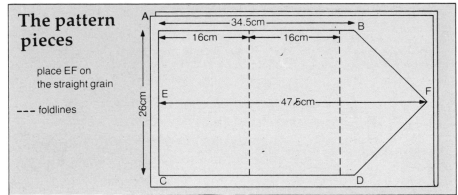

The pattern pieces

place EF on the straight grain

--- foldlines

on sloping edges, and between two tent stitch rows on back edge. Place bag pieces right sides together. Stitch all round with 1cm/½in seam, stitching close to needlepoint on flap and leaving short edge open for turning. Turn to right side and press carefully. To give the bag extra stiffening, cut buckram to fit exactly inside

and slip into place. Tack round bag edges, turning in 1cm/½in allowance on open edge. Topstitch round needlepoint flap inside tent stitch row and along short edge. Fold bag into shape, bringing short edge up to base of needlepoint, and stitch side seams close to the edge by hand or machine. Attach press stud fastening. Remove all tacking.

---

canvas threads, and the width, 54.) Following the chart, beginning in lower right corner, work the design of diagonal bands, using two strands of crewel wool in the needle or one strand of Persian yarn. Work in oblong cross stitch (with a centre catching stitch) and crossed corners. Fill in each oblong gap along the edges with two regular cross stitches over two threads. The oblong stitches are all in blue, and the crossed corners in alternating shades of pink and burgundy.

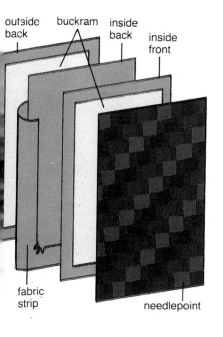

outside back   buckram   inside back   inside front

fabric strip   needlepoint

Making up the case
Block needlepoint, or press, face downwards, on a well-padded ironing board. Cut four pieces of buckram (for stiffening) measuring same as stitched area (16.5cm×9cm/6½in×3½in). Cut three pieces of fabric measuring 18.5cm×11cm/7¼in×4¼in, and one strip measuring 2.5cm×40cm/1in×16in.
Inside and outside back, inside front Cover one side of three of the buckram pieces with the fabric, turning 1cm/½in to the other side all round, clipping corners slightly. Pull fabric tight and stick down round the 1cm/½in turning, handling fabric carefully so that no adhesive spoils the right side. Trim canvas border round needlepoint to 1cm/½in. Lay canvas on one side of the other piece of buckram and stick the border down on the other side. Neaten both short ends of fabric strip with a 1cm/½in turning.

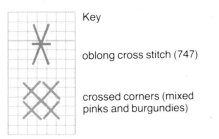

Key

oblong cross stitch (747)

crossed corners (mixed pinks and burgundies)

Assembling the back Lay outside back wrong side up. Lay right side of strip on buckram, 2cm/¾in down from top edge on each side, and overlapping so that 1.5cm/⅝in of the strip protrudes all round. Stick. Lay inside back on top, wrong sides together, so that strip protrudes between layers, except on top edge, and stick in place.
Assembling back and front Lay inside front on assembled back, right side of inside front to inside back. Wrap the protruding strip tightly over edge of inside front and stick in place. Lay the needlepoint piece in place on inside front and stick.

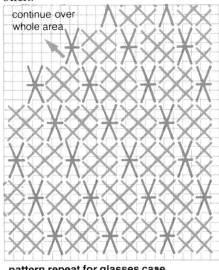

continue over whole area

pattern repeat for glasses case

CHAPTER 6

Working on a frame using a range of sampler stitches

This chapter give you guidance on choosing and using frames for needlepoint – a good idea for neat stitchery. Frame up your canvas and start stitching the sampler cushion cover – each area of the beautiful design is worked in a different stitch.

Although it is not essential, a frame keeps needlepoint evenly stretched – and you will find it is much easier to count threads and keep work neat when canvas is taut. The finished piece will also need less blocking.

It is always advisable to use a frame for pieces incorporating different stitches, diagonal stitches, couched threads, beads, laid threads in silk or stranded cotton, and for pulled-thread work.

Choose the type of frame most suitable for you and the space available – if possible, one that allows you to use both hands.

Artists' stretcher bars

These are the least expensive and most widely available type of frame. Bars come in pairs, and lengths from 25cm/9¾in upwards. Buy two pairs, one about 10cm/4in longer than the width and one about 10cm/4in longer than the depth of the design (not the canvas), you are working. For example, a design 25cm×30cm/9¾in ×11¾in on a canvas 35cm×40cm/ 13¾in×15¾in would need one pair of 35cm/13¾in and one pair 40cm/ 15¾in bars – they slot together at the corners. The canvas is mounted as tightly as possible, with drawing pins so it can be re-tightened as work progresses. To work with two hands, rest the frame on the edge of a table or the arm of a chair.

Below: Frames for needlepoint come in various different shapes and sizes.

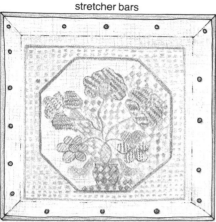
stretcher bars

Ring frame

This type comes in several sizes and consists of two hoops that fit one inside the other. A frame with a stand is best because it leaves both of your hands free. Choose from a knee or table stand, or table clamp, according to how you prefer to work. The knee/table stand frame is the most convenient to work with because the canvas can be mounted in seconds, so you are not tempted to work some areas without the frame (it really does show).

To mount the canvas, place it over the inner ring, place the outer ring on top and tighten the side screw to hold the work taut.

Sometimes, when working a large canvas, you will need to cover stitches with the ring. Wool yarn is unaffected, but when working with fine, fragile threads, it is best to cover the work with tissue paper before mounting on the frame, and tear away the paper just over the area being worked.

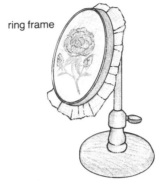
ring frame

Slate frame

This square or rectangular stretcher frame comes in several types and sizes, from 45cm/17¾in square upwards. It consists of taped rollers top and bottom and adjustable side stretchers with either screws, ratchets, pegs or split pins to hold the taped bars apart – giving the correct size and tension for the work.

The canvas is stitched to the tape on the top and bottom rollers and laced to the side bars (so it must not be wider than they are).

If you choose a slate frame drilled to fit a floor stand, you can buy a stand (now or later) which will make it easier to work with both hands.

Travelling frame

Sometimes called a rotating frame, this works on a similar principle to the slate frame. After stitching the work to the taped rollers, these can be rolled and fixed so that only the area being worked is exposed. This frame comes in two sizes, 30cm/11¾in square and 30cm×45cm/11¾in×17¾in.

Stitching on a frame

Have your right hand under the canvas to guide your weaker (left) hand which stays on top. If you are left-handed, simply reverse these positions. Pass the needle between your hands as if it were a weaving shuttle, making the stitches with a stabbing motion.

Renaissance Garden sampler cushion

The design of this beautiful cushion – worked in a stunning combination of coffee and cream crewel wool and stranded cotton – is based on the geometric layout of a French chateau's formal garden – each flowerbed is worked in a different stitch and bordered by cross stitch hedges and square mosaic stitch paths.

You will need

1½×25g hanks Appleton's crewel wool in off-white (992)
1×25g hank in fawn (952)
7 skeins Twilley's Lystra stranded cotton in camel (836) and 8 in cream (843)
2 tapestry needles size 20, 1 size 22
Large blunt rug needle *or* curved needle
40cm/½yd piece of white 14-gauge mono canvas (narrow width)
Pencil *or* grey Nepo waterproof marker
2 pairs of 40cm/16in stretcher bars *or* a slate frame (if possible)
40cm/½yd fawn or cream heavy

backing fabric (any width)
35cm/14in square cushion pad
Working hints Always keep the canvas selvedge at the side when working. You may turn the canvas completely upside down to reach an area more easily, but never turn it on its side. This rule helps you to work all the stitches in the right direction.
Remember that it is always better to come up in an empty hole, if possible. Use the key to the chart to find out which thread, shade and how many strands to use.
Needles Two size 20 needles are recommended, because in areas of the design where you are using two different colours or threads together, it is easier to have a needle for each.
The large rug needle or curved needle is used for smoothing out stranded cotton stitches before pulling them down on to the canvas. Hold it in the hand which is not holding the main needle, and make the stitches over it, gently

easing it out as you pull the stitch tight.
Crewel wool When working with the uncut 25g hanks of crewel wool, cut each hank through once at each end to obtain threads of the correct length.
Stranded cotton This thread needs 'stripping' before you begin stitching, to make it lie smoothly and give the best canvas coverage. Cut a piece 50cm/20in long and pull the six individual strands apart. Lay them flat, side by side, before gathering together and threading the needle with the number of strands recommended for the particular stitch.
Beginning threads When working a needlepoint sampler with different stitches, you will find yourself constantly beginning new threads in different parts of the canvas. There may be no stitching nearby (for anchoring the thread) so make a knot and insert the needle at the front of the canvas, fairly near the point where you are working.

Above: Pale and subtle colouring in this elegant cushion gives maximum effect to the texture of the stitches. The soft sheen comes from the stranded cotton which has been combined with the wool.

When the knot is eventually reached by stitching, cut if off close to the canvas. The stitches will have caught the 'tail' firmly on the back. Finish off threads in the usual way, running through the back of several stitches.

Marking the canvas
Cut canvas to a 40cm/16in square. Bind the edges with masking tape and mark the centre.
Mark the design on to the canvas by counting threads – each square on the chart equals two threads. Use the pencil or waterproof marker and work outwards from the centre. Each line on the chart corresponds to a line of *holes* on the canvas. To mark straight lines, simply place the point of the pencil or marker in the channel between two threads and run it along for the required number of threads, counting each one as the pencil or marker bumps over it. If you use a pencil, give the canvas a good rub with white kitchen paper before you start to work or some of the graphite may come off.

Beginning to stitch the cushion
First, work all the paths between the blocks in square mosaic stitch. Now work the hedges round each flowerbed in padded cross stitch. Lay the padding stitch with three strands of crewel wool and work the top cross stitch over two threads in stranded cotton using the 22 needle, so that the wool shows through. Once you have worked the paths and hedges, the working order is not crucial. If you work outwards from the centre, your hands will not rest on areas you have already stitched.

Key to chart
The paths are shown in yellow, the hedges fawn and the flowerbeds salmon on the chart opposite. Use the photograph above as a guide to the colour scheme.
Paths: Square mosaic stitch 2 strands crewel wool.
Hedges: Padded cross stitch Padding stitch: 3 strands crewel wool, cross stitch: 3 strands stranded cotton (22 needle).
A1 Diagonal tent 6 strands stranded cotton with single Leviathan stitch in centre of square: 3 strands crewel wool (large cross), 6 strands stranded cotton (upright cross).
A2 Diagonal tent 6 strands stranded cotton, four Leviathan stitches in square (threads as A1).
B Crossed corners Large cross: 3 strands crewel wool, small crossing stitches: 6 strands stranded cotton.

C1 and C2 Milanese stitch 6 strands stranded cotton, 2nd row: 6 strands stranded cotton, reverse diagram for C2.

D1 and D2 Oriental stitch 6 strands stranded cotton, 2nd row: 6 strands stranded cotton, reverse diagram for D2.

E Double brick stitch Work over 4 threads, 6 strands stranded cotton. (Work horizontally.)

F Chequer stitch Diagonal tent: 3 strands crewel wool, boxes: 6 strands stranded cotton.

G Ray stitch Diagonal tent: 3 strands crewel wool, rays: 6 strands stranded cotton.

H Cushion stitch Alternately 6 strands stranded cotton, 3 strands crewel wool.

I Small waffle stitch Alternately 6 strands stranded cotton, 3 strands crewel wool.

J Eyelets and crossed corners Eyelets: 6 strands stranded cotton, crossed corners: 6 strands stranded cotton.

All the new stitches are described in detail below and on the following four pages.

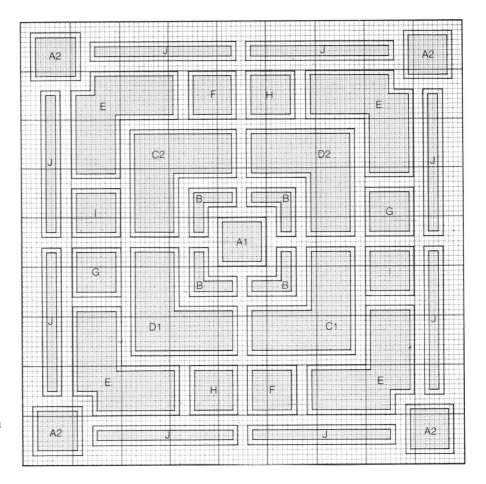

New stitches for the sampler cushion

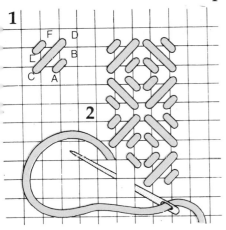

Square mosaic stitch
This stitch is composed of small blocks of three stitches each.
1 Begin with a short tent stitch over one canvas intersection (A–B), a longer stitch above it over two canvas intersections (C–D). Finish off the block with another short tent stitch (E–F). All three stitches slope in the same direction.
2 Adjacent blocks should slope in alternate directions, forming a chequerboard effect. The blocks will share the same canvas holes along the edges.

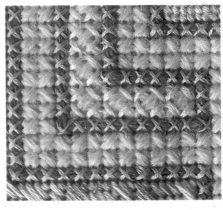

Square mosaic stitch is a useful filler.

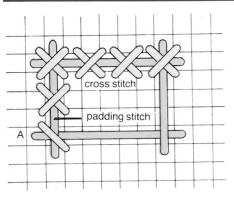

Padded cross stitch
To give a raised and decorative effect to cross stitch, work it over a straight 'padding' thread laid along the canvas in advance.
The diagram shows you how to turn corners with padding stitches, outlining an oblong shape, beginning at point A.
Work regular cross stitch over two threads, using a contrasting thread for the best effect.

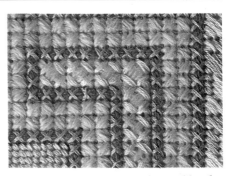

Padded cross stitch makes a good border.

Chequer stitch

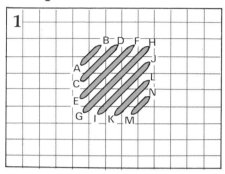

This stitch is formed of square boxes, as its name suggests. It looks very effective worked in two different threads.
1 Work diagonal straight stitches over one, two, three, four, three, two and one canvas intersections as shown. Leave alternate squares free.

Ray stitch

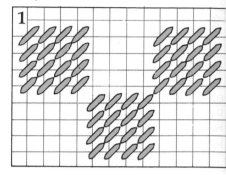

2 Now work the alternate squares in diagonal tent stitch, with the stitches all sloping in the same direction. The outer stitches on this box share a hole with stitches in the four adjacent straight stitch boxes. The boxes are alternated throughout.

This very attractive stitch is also based on square units.
1 Work a series of square blocks of diagonal tent stitch, four stitches wide and four stitches deep. Leave alternating squares free.

Cushion stitch

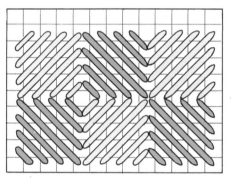

This stitch is very effective when light catches the alternating blocks of diagonal stitches.
For each 'square', work seven diagonal stitches, with a central one over four canvas intersections, and three more on each side, graduating in size over three, two and one intersections.
Each hole along the edge of a square will be shared by two stitches.

Eyelets

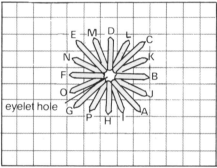

eyelet hole

Often used in pulled thread work, this stitch incorporates 16 straight stitches, all converging in the same hole at the centre. If you wish to create a lacy look enlarge the central hole first with a large rug needle. Follow the stitch order carefully from the diagram, so that no threads run across the hole on the back of the work.

Leviathan stitch

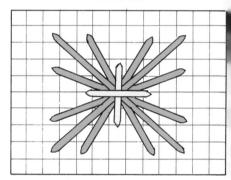

This is similar to triple cross stitch but the long stitches are worked over eight canvas intersections (instead of eight threads) causing the whole stitch to lie at a different angle. And the small central cross stitch becomes an upright. Working this in a contrasting thread looks most effective.

An alternate colourway

Stitch the Renaissance Garden cushion in any colour. The one in the picture opposite has been worked in blue and cream using the same stitches given with the chart on pages 36 and 37. By working the paths and hedges in two shades of blue crewel wool the whole emphasis of the design is changed giving a more vibrant look to the pattern when compared with the cream and fawn colour scheme.

You will need
1½ × 25g Appleton's crewel wool in pale blue (743)
1 × 25g Appleton's crewel wool in dark blue (746)
7 skeins Twilley's Lystra stranded cotton in blue (641) and 8 in cream (843)

Starting to stitch
Try out each new stitch on a spare piece of canvas and make sure you can work it confidently before filling the appropriate area on the canvas. Square and diagonal pattern stitches like these are wonderfully versatile, neatly filling geometric shapes and creating fascinating textural effects. Experiment by using two different colours in one stitch or work in cotton and wool of the same shade.
Use the picture opposite and the detail on page 41 as a colour guide.

Small waffle stitch

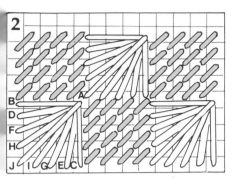

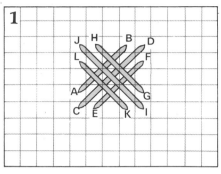

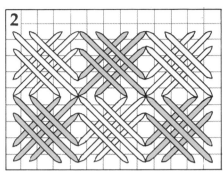

2 Now, in the alternating squares, work the blocks of ray-like stitches in the suggested order (A-B, A-C and so on). Each one uses the same hole (A) in the upper right corner, and the other end of each stitch shares a hole with one of the tent stitches in the next block.

Another stitch which forms a square pattern.
1 Work three stitches over 3, 4 and 3 canvas intersections in one direction and then work three stitches over 3, 4 and 3 threads in the opposite direction, on top.

2 Continue working in square blocks with all the top stitches sloping in the same direction. Two different shades or types of thread can be used very successfully.

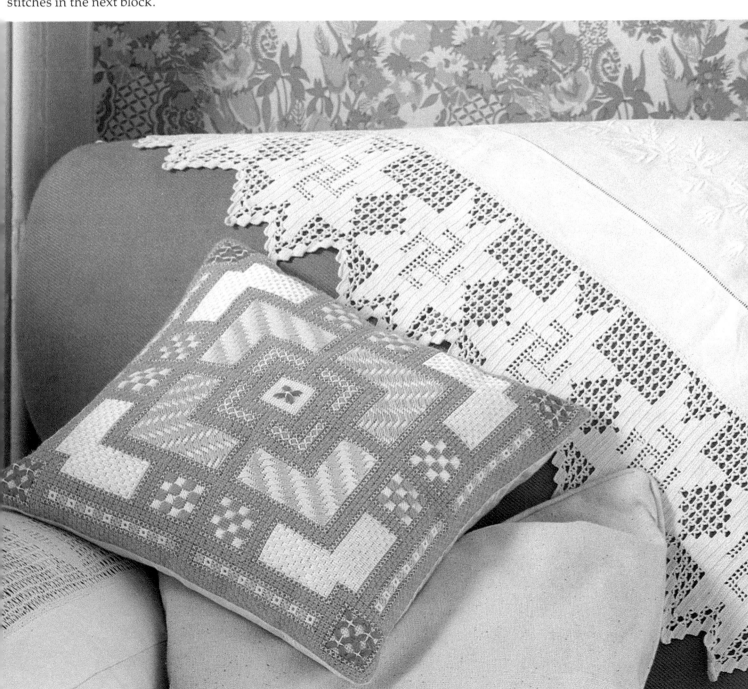

Milanese stitch

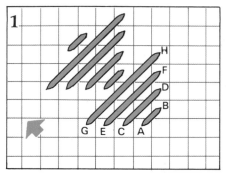

Oriental stitch

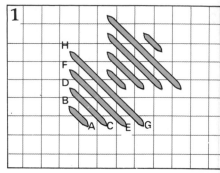

This striking stitch forms a diagonal pattern of triangular arrowheads running in alternate directions, making a good all-over zigzag design.

1 Begin with a tent stitch over one canvas intersection (A-B), then work over two, three and four intersections in turn (C-D, E-F, G-H) to make the triangle. Begin the

next arrowhead with another short tent stitch centred over the longest stitch of the first arrowhead, and continue working diagonally upwards.

2 Reverse the direction of the arrowheads for the downward row. Working alternate rows in different colours creates an even more attractive pattern.

This pretty variation of Milanese stitch looks like steps.

1 Begin with a row of Milanese stitch arrowheads running diagonally in whichever direction you wish to work.

2 For the second row, change threads if you wish, and make groups of three even stitches over two canvas intersections, sloping in

Finishing the sampler cushion

Continue to refer to the key to the working chart on pages 36–37.

Milanese stitch
Areas C1 and C2, which are diagonally opposite to each other, are worked in Milanese stitch. Work the stitches over a rug needle to keep the stranded cottons smooth. To work area C1, begin in the outer corner with a short stitch and work first row of triangles in one colour. Work downward row of triangles above in second colour stranded cotton. Near the outside edge, work compensation stitches of irregular length to obtain a straight edge. When you begin the second colour

thread, work some pattern stitches in the correct position first (begin at the dot in the diagram), then go back and fill in the compensation stitches. The diagram shows you how to deal with the inner corners as well as the outer ones.

Oriental stitch
Now work areas D1 and D2 in Oriental stitch, reversing the stitch diagram for D2. Begin at the outer corners as for the Milanese stitch and use two needles – one for each shade of cotton.
To work the row containing compensation stitches, begin at the dot in the diagram.

Double brick stitch
Fill the areas marked E with double brick stitch (which is worked in the same way as brick stitch, but with the stitches in identical pairs), worked horizontally. If the work is not on a frame, you may turn it sideways in order to work the brick stitch vertically.
To obtain a straight edge, work the compensation stitches over two threads, as shown. Add these after working the complete row nearest the edge.

Working the small squares
Now work the squares of chequer stitch, ray stitch, and small waffle stitch, taking care to slope all the

Milanese stitch

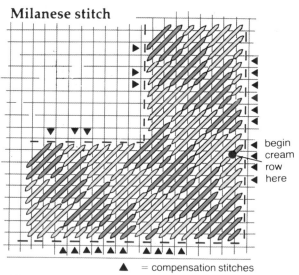

begin cream row here

Oriental stitch

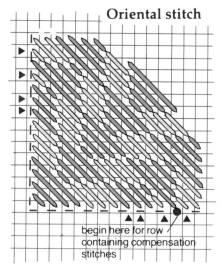

begin here for row containing compensation stitches

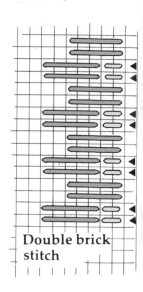

Double brick stitch

▲ = compensation stitches

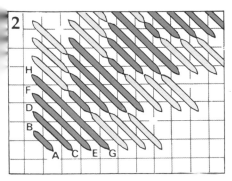

2

the same dirction as the first row stitches. Work them into the same holes as the ends of the three smallest stitches in each triangle. When you have done this along the upper and lower edges of the Milanese stitch, you will see shapes developing into which you work the next row of arrowheads pointing in the opposite direction.

Above: Geometric designs are ideal for samplers: each area contains a new stitch.

stitches in the correct direction in relation to the top edge.
When stitching the areas marked H (cushion stitch), run a diagonal thread across the two squares to be worked in stranded cotton before adding the stitches, to give extra body. The diagram shows you how to run the thread from the lower left corner of one square to the upper right corner of the one diagonally nearest.

Crossed corners and eyelets
All the long bars marked J are worked as rows of alternating crossed corners and eyelets.
Work all the crossed corners first (beginning each one at top right –

see dots), leaving a gap four threads wide between each. The crossed corners should be at the inside ends of each bar.
To make a pretty lacy effect, enlarge the eyelet holes as described.

The finishing touches
Finally, add the striking Leviathan stitches – one in the centre of area A1 and four in each square marked A2.
Work them on top of the tent stitch background already worked. Each stitch spans eight canvas threads in either direction. The diagrams show you exactly where to place stitches. Check the work for any missed stitches and remove from the frame

– if you are using one. Block and set the canvas, making sure that the edges are straight.

Making up
Trim the canvas border to 1cm/½in. Cut the backing fabric to a square 34cm×34cm/13½in×13½in (the same size as canvas).
With right sides together, machine stitch three sides of cover, taking a 1cm/½in seam. Stitch fourth side, leaving a central gap of 20cm/7¼in. Trim corners, turn and insert cushion pad through opening. Slipstitch opening neatly.

Cushion stitch

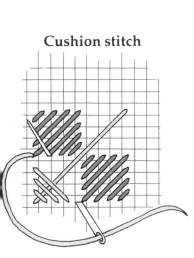

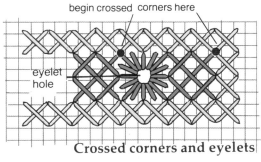

begin crossed corners here

eyelet hole

Crossed corners and eyelets

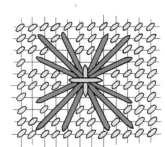

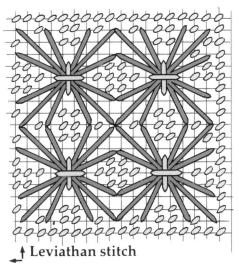

Leviathan stitch

Design ideas for sampler cushions

These three cushions use patterns based on diamond and lattice shapes to evoke the delicate tracery you might find in a Moorish mosque. A subtle mixture of wools with matt and shiny cotton threads, together with a few ribbons for highlights, have been used. Some of the stitches allow the white mono canvas to show through which keeps the overall effect light and lacy. Others use the pulled thread technique described in detail on pages 64–65. Details on how to insert a ribbon border such as that

shown on the cushion on the left are given on page 57.

The square cushion in the foreground has a Gothic Florentine border framing the design worked in all the colours used in the embroidery. The chart for this together with information on how to work a variety of border designs is given on page 79. Plan your own geometric design on a sheet of graph paper first and then transfer it accurately to the canvas using a pencil or waterproof marker. You will find the stitches given in

Above: Instructions for making up your needlepoint into a cushion are given on page 25. Choose a toning backing made from a plain furnishing fabric.

chapters 5, 6, 10, 11, 12 and 14 particularly useful for this type of needlepoint.

Always work any design outlines first to set the pattern; it is then easy to fill in the diamonds, triangles, etc, with the appropriate stitches. The cushions above will start you off with some design ideas.

CHAPTER 7

Pile stitches add a third dimension

Needlepoint stitches which give a soft pile effect are fun to do and cover the canvas quickly. Once you have mastered the three shown here, plus three new background stitches, you can make an appealing panda picture for a favourite child.

Some needlepoint stitches produce a raised pile, creating a rug-like effect. In fact these stitches are sometimes used to make needlepoint rugs – the loops formed can be left uncut, or trimmed evenly to make tufts. They can also be used for any project where you want a raised texture, for abstract designs with textural variations, or for novelty effects in designs such as animal pictures.

The three pile stitches introduced here should all be worked in horizontal rows from left to right and upwards over the canvas. This is because the pile tends to lie downwards once it has been stitched, covering the few rows of canvas threads underneath. If you find it tricky keeping the loops uniform, work over a knitting needle chosen to give the required size.

This chapter also shows you three new textured stitches, useful for building up backgrounds in pictorial needlepoint.

Below: Stitch this brightly-coloured needlepoint picture or design your own using simple shapes.

Three pile stitches

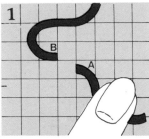

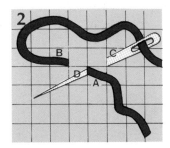

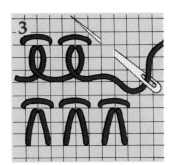

Single knotted stitch
This stitch gives a dense pile effect. The loops can be left uncut, cut through or trimmed short.
1 Insert the needle at A, leaving a short length of yarn anchored by the left thumb. Bring the needle up at B (1 canvas thread up and 2 to the left).

2 Reinsert the needle at C (3 threads to the right of B) and bring it out again at D, pulling firmly to make a tight knot. Make the next stitch, leaving a loop between the two stitches.

3 Continue along the row in this way, so that each tight horizontal stitch shares a hole with the next one. Try to keep the loops regular. Leave a free row of horizontal canvas thread between each row of stitches (leave two for a less dense pile).

Velvet stitch
This stitch gives a pile similar to that of an Oriental carpet.
1 Bring the needle out at A; re-insert it at B (2 threads to the right and 2 up), bring it out again at A. Now re-insert the needle at B leaving a loop of thread and bring it out under the loop at C (2 threads down). Re-

Three useful textured stitches

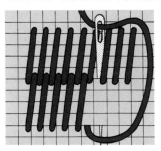

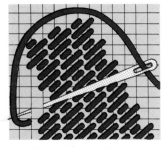

Encroaching gobelin stitch
This stitch is closely worked and gives an

attractively textured background useful for colour shading effects – each row of stitches overlaps slightly with the rows above and below it. Start at the top of the area and work each stitch over five horizontal canvas threads, and diagonally over one vertical one as shown. Work backwards and forwards in rows.

Cashmere stitch
Another useful texture stitch – this one looks almost like woven fabric

with a diagonal grain. Work in units of three stitches over 1, 2, and 2 canvas threads, progressing diagonally down the canvas by moving one thread to the right after each three-stitch unit. On the return journey, work diagonally upwards, this time moving one thread to the left each time.

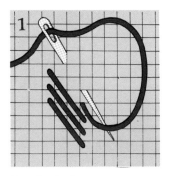

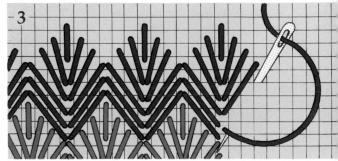

Leaf stitch
This pretty stitch forms a series of 'leaves' on the surface of the canvas. Use it as an all-over texture or in leaf and tree pictorial designs.
Each leaf consists of 11 straight stitches – three at

each side and five fanned out at the top.
1 Beginning at the base of the leaf, follow the working order given in the diagram. The three stitches on each side of the leaf lie directly in line with one another.

2 Continue round the top of the leaf. Note that all the central ends of the stitches lie along the same vertical row of canvas holes.
3 When the leaf is complete, begin the next one six holes to the right

(or left) of it, so that the side stitches of the leaves share the same holes. For an all-over texture, begin the leaves for the row above in the hole where two top side stitches converge.

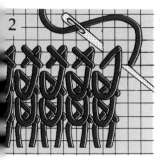

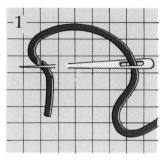

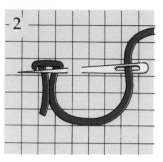

nsert it at D (2 threads up
nd 2 to the left, bringing
t out again at C ready
or the next stitch.
. Continue working
upwards over the canvas,
und when the whole area
o be worked is covered,
cut through the centre of
each loop to form the pile,
rimming them evenly to
he desired length.

Rya stitch
Dense, overlapping
loops make this a good
'special effects' stitch.
1 Holding the end of the
yarn on the right side of
the canvas, pass the
needle from right to left
under a vertical canvas
thread and pull through.
Make the next stitch in
the next thread to the
right, pulling tightly.

2 Pass the needle under
the next vertical thread to
the right, pull through
forming a loop and hold
this loop in place with
your thumb while you
make the next stitch
under the next vertical
canvas thread. Pull
through tightly to secure
the loop. With the next
stitch, form the next
loop.

3 Continue along the
row, alternately forming
loops and tight stitches
and keeping all the loops
even. Work the next row
in the horizontal line of
holes just above this one.

Playful pandas nursery picture

The colourful needlepoint nursery
picture of pandas shown on page 43
will delight any young child and re-
main a favourite for many years to
come. It's fun to work and includes
several different stitches which bring
the picture alive with their interesting textures – fluffy clouds and pandas, leafy trees and daisy-scattered
grass.

You will need
50cm/½yd white 14-gauge mono
  canvas
Appletons crewel wool:
5 small skeins white (991), 3 skeins
  each black (993), grass green 1, 3
  and 5 (251, 253, 255)
2 skeins each grass green 6 (256),
  sky blue 1 and 3 (561, 563)
1 skein each red fawn 5 (305), iron
  grey 7 (967), scarlet 3 (503), bright
  yellow 2 (552), royal blue 4 (824)
  and turquoise 4 (524)
Tapestry needle size 22
Nepo waterproof marker

Preparing the canvas
Bind the edges of the canvas with
masking tape and mark the centre.
Boldly trace the design outlines
from the life-size photograph
(overleaf) on to tracing paper.
Centre the canvas over the tracing
and re-trace the outlines with a

waterproof marker.
If possible, mount the canvas on
stretcher bars or a slate frame.

Working the design
As far as possible, stitch from the
centre of the picture outwards, but
leaving the two pandas till last. Use
three strands of crewel wool

throughout except for the lake area
where you should use four strands.
Lake Gobelin filling stitch over six
threads.
Bees Tent stitch.

*Below: For a smaller project, pick out a
panda motif from the picture, and add a
plain, primary colour background.*

Trace pattern for panda picture

Centre field Cashmere stitch.
Left hand trees Trunks in tent stitch, foliage in leaf stitch.
Sky Encroaching gobelin stitch, becoming darker towards the top.
Clouds Single knotted stitch, cut to a short pile when complete.
Left hand field background Work this area in Milanese stitch in a single colour.
Right hand field background Using the same green, change to brick stitch.
Ball Continental tent stitch.
Right hand tree This tree has a cross stitch trunk and rya stitch foliage – leave rya stitch loopy.

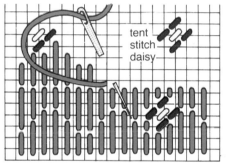

Working the foreground field First scatter the foreground with tent stitch daisies, each one worked as five stitches – a central yellow one and four surrounding white ones. Fill in the remaining area with graduated straight stitch in a zigzag pattern as shown.
Pandas The eyes, noses and bamboo shoots are all worked in tent stitch. Use tent stitch for the inside of the paws too. The fluffy bodies of both pandas are worked in velvet stitch, cut to a short pile.

Finishing off
Check your work for missed stitches and take it off the frame. It's not a good idea to dampen this design as black wool can run when used on white canvas, but these stitches should hardly distort the canvas.
Stretch the canvas tightly over a piece of strong card or hardboard and lace firmly at the back (see page 27, Mounting the picture). Use a purchased frame to frame the picture or have it framed professionally.

Left: Use this lifesize photograph as your trace pattern. Remember that pile stitches tend to overlap the outlines.

CHAPTER 8

Four textured stitches

*Complete your collection of textural needlepoint stitches
with the four shown here. Make a cheerful
picture of a plump black and white cat sitting on a busily-
patterned carpet. A well-designed picture
succeeds even with this many colours and stitches.*

Needlepoint pictures can be fun t
work and provide the perfect chanc
to try out unfamiliar stitches to buil
up interesting textures.
The four new stitches, shown righ
have been incorporated into the co
ourful domestic scene that makes u
the enchanting picture above.
Full working instructions are give
in this chapter plus a close-up of th
actual-size picture to use as a trac
pattern, instead of having to draw
from a graph.

Four new textured stitches

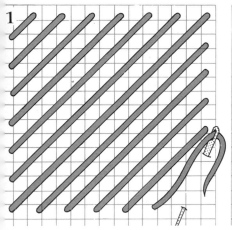

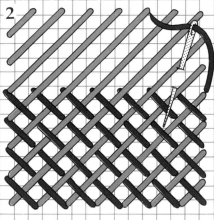

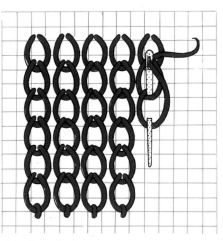

Web stitch
This firm, all-over texture stitch gives a woven effect when worked in two colours.
1 With the first colour in the needle, lay a series of diagonal threads across the canvas, so that they run across each alternate line of holes. The thread does not pass through the canvas except at the edge of the stitching area.

Left: Pictures like this jolly cat in an interior are fun to stitch in several different textured stitches.

2 With the second colour, work stitches diagonally in the opposite direction.
Work stitches in horizontal rows like half cross stitches but only working into every alternate hole, to 'tie' the long threads in place. Where these stitches meet in one hole, make sure the long, laid thread runs between them.
No stitch should 'tie' the same thread as the stitch before or following it.

Chain stitch
Needlepoint chain stitch is worked in exactly the same way as on fabric, except that stitches are regulated by the canvas threads.
Working vertically, bring the needle up in the first hole, loop the thread and hold with a finger. Re-insert the needle in the same hole and bring it up two holes further down, catching the loop of thread as you pull it through. Make the loop for the next stitch, and so on.
At the end of a row, hold the final loop in place with a catching stitch.

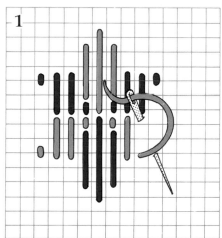

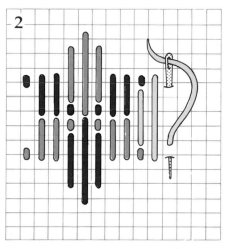

Dutch stitch
This stitch, useful for all-over patterns, is formed of interlocking stars. Begin each stitch by working an oblong cross stitch horizontally – that is, spanning four vertical canvas threads and two horizontal. To finish off, work a single vertical straight stitch over four horizontal threads, in the centre to complete the star. The ends of these straight stitches should share holes with the ends of adjoining stars, as shown.

Interlocking diamond stitch
Another 'pattern' stitch formed of closely-interlocking geometric shapes. Six diamonds make a six-pointed star. You can either work each 'star' in one colour, or use different colours for individual diamonds.
1 Work the upright diamonds as straight stitches over 4, 6 and 4 threads. The sideways diamonds which interlock with them are worked over 1, 3, 3, and 1 threads.

2 Having completed a star shape, work an upright diamond in the space created by two of the sideways diamonds. You need another upright diamond and three more sideways diamonds to complete the second star.

Contented cat picture

Stitch yourself a purring pussycat sitting in a colourful roomscape, and getting into mischief with a ball of wool! As well as the cat, the window scene, wallpaper and carpet are all fascinating to work. There are lots of different stitches to hold your interest as well as a colourful mixture of different threads – soft, matt cotton, stranded cotton, pearl cotton and tapestry wool. A web stitch 'frame' finishes the design; choose neutrals for this, to enhance the picture.
(Note that you need three sizes of tapestry needle to suit the various threads.)

You will need

28cm×36cm/11in×14in piece of 16-gauge mono canvas
Tapestry needles size 20, 22, 24
Tracing paper
Thick black felt-tip pen
Waterproof marker

for the cat
1 skein each DMC tapestry wool in 7192 noir, 7285 blanc, 7911 and 7604
1 skein bright green stranded embroidery wool
Oddments of silver metallic thread for whiskers (Twilleys Goldfingering is a suitable choice)

for the window frame and border
2 skeins each DMC cotton Retors à broder in 2938 and 2939

for the wallpaper
1 skein each DMC pearl cotton No 5 in 437, 223, 920, 301, 841 and ecru

for the carpet
1 skein each DMC stranded cotton in 900, 352, 741, 321, 3041 and 725

for the sky
1 skein each DMC cotton Retors à broder in 2825, 2826, 2798, 2799, 2828, 2800 and 2933

For the hedge
1 skein each DMC cotton Retors à broder in 1956, 2907 and 2957

Working the needlepoint design

Mark the centre of the piece of canvas and bind the edges with masking tape.
Trace off the main design outlines using a thick, black felt-tip. Lay the canvas centrally over the design and transfer the outlines to the canvas with a waterproof marker. Mount the canvas on stretcher bars or a frame if possible.
Stitching the cat Use tapestry wool and a size 20 needle. Work in vertical straight stitches, using the ends of stitches to define the contours of the cat. Using this heavier yarn makes the cat stand out well against the patterned carpet and wallpaper.

Stitching the carpet Using a size 22 needle and stranded cotton, stitch the busy, multi-coloured pattern on the carpet in interlocking diamond stitch.
Strip down the stranded cotton into separate strands before using it and work each stitch with six strands in the needle, then with another six so that each stitch has the weight of 12 threads. This gives good canvas coverage.
Stitching the wallpaper Use Dutch stitch and a size 24 needle to fill the wallpaper area. Random shades of pearl cotton form the all-over interlocking design. They complement the carpet colours, but are more subdued and the difference in thread texture enhances this effect.
Stitching the sky Stitch the sky in blended blues from light to dark, using encroaching gobelin stitch worked over four horizontal threads. Change the thread colour

after each row, shading from dark at the top to light at the bottom.
Stitching the hedge The green hedge outside the window is stitched in three different greens using Hungarian stitch. Work small random patches in each of the colours.
Stitching the basket of flowers First work the basket in straight stitch, then fill in with multi-coloured flowers formed by mixing together freely embroidered French knots, eyelets and double cross stitches. Add touches of green for the leaves.
Stitching the ball of wool Rows of chain stitch make a realistic ball of wool. Work several vertical rows to form the main ball shape, then add a few rows worked diagonally across the ball and a wandering thread festooned around the cat. Use one strand of stranded wool and a size 24 needle.
Stitching the frame Web stitch in two colours makes an effective border. Use the beige soft cotton for the laid threads and the brown for the tying stitches.
Lastly, using silver, add the highlights in the cat's eyes (French knots) and the whiskers (straight stitches). Take the work off the frame or stretcher bars, mount and frame if you wish.

Left: There's a wealth of different colours and threads in the cat picture.
Right: Use this actual-size photo as your working chart.

CHAPTER 9

Freestyle needlepoint for subtle tones and textures

Try your hand at freestyle stitchery, even if you're not a dab hand with a paintbrush. This technique relies on simplicity of design, enriched by mixing textures and materials. Stitch a beautiful square picture with subtly mixed tones and a random border.

To build up a freestyle design, use a mixture of stitches, threads and colours carefully chosen to reflect the quality of the subject. Decide where you want solid blocks of colour and where subtle tonal mixtures are required, where you need texture or smoothness, and where you need matt wools, or the slight sheen of silk or cotton.

Choosing stitches

Different textures and the way the interact play an important part. French knots, a stitch usually associated with embroidery on fabric, ca be suitable for natural foliage an flowers on canvas. In contrast, sati stitch or encroaching Gobelin stitc work well as flat surfaces – wood o bricks, for instance. Tent stitch is al ways a useful standby.

Consider whether your stitches ar intended for the foreground or back ground of the needlepoint. Flatte stitches make shapes recede into th background while textured stitche appear to move to the front of picture. Used with discretion, thi technique helps to create three dimensional effects, as in the centr

Interesting stitches for freestyle needlepoint

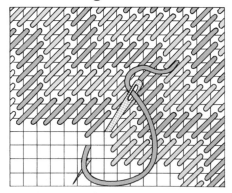

Byzantine stitch
This stitch consists of diagonal satin stitches worked over two, three or four canvas intersections, forming a zigzag pattern of steps. The finished effect looks like woven fabric. This stitch is quick to work and a useful background filling.

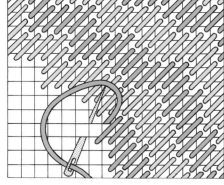

Random Byzantine stitch
For freestyle designs, stitch in a less regular way. Try working over two canvas intersections for a more detailed effect. Work out an irregular step pattern across the motif, keeping all stitches the same length, then repeat to fill the area.

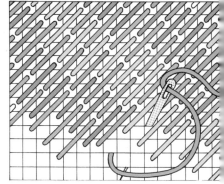

Random Gobelin filling stitch
Work as Gobelin filling stitch but this time diagonally over odd numbers of intersections.
Work a row of level stitches (with a row of empty holes between each stitch for the next row).
Occasionally, move the stitch one hole to the left or right and make the other rows follow suit.

Freestyle garden picture with border

This beautiful picture with its subtly-toned central landscape and riotously coloured border uses a combination of stitches and materials. The square panel in the centre of the picture gives the impression of looking through a camera viewfinder. The colours are mixed and the stitches more highly textured, whereas in the rest of the picture they are flatter. Stretch the finished needlepoint over hardboard before framing but do not place it under glass.

You will need
33cm/13in square of white 18-gauge mono canvas
Coats Anchor stranded cotton, 1 skein each in 1212, 0212, 0851, 0899, 0210, 0216, 0218, 0245, 0261, 0258, 0888, 0264, 0266, 0281, 0400, 0398, 0397, 1087, 1214, 063, 096, 0107, 0108, 095, 0349
Coats Anchor tapisserie wool, 1 skein each in 096, 0105
Small pale green and pink glass beads, about 80 in each colour

Tapestry needle size 18
Crewel needle size 10
Square or rectangular frame, or stretcher bars
Masking tape
Waterproof marker
Tracing paper

Preparing the canvas
Bind the edges of the canvas with masking tape and mark the centre. Trace the main design outlines on to the tracing paper using a thick,

section of the square picture. This represents a more detailed view of the scene, so massed French knots add heavy texture to this area. Smoother stitches in the rest of the picture area look more distant.

Canvas has a regular, grid-like structure, normally reflected by the stitches worked on it. Experiment by ignoring the grid, working mixtures of random stitches in all directions, combining colours and threads. The border of the square picture shown below is a perfect example of disguising the canvas grid.

Using borders

Borders work well on freestyle stitchery. They help to balance and frame pictorial designs that have no geo-metric structure of their own and are pleasing to the eye. Careful colour and stitch choice can co-ordinate the different elements of the main design. Border patterns can be in random or geometric designs, or a combination of the two.

Colours, threads and canvas

Choosing colours and materials is one of the most exciting parts of this type of needlepoint. Select several tones of the same colour rather than unrelated colours.

Colour mixing To capture the subtle colours of Nature successfully, try mixing and blending threads as you would if using paint. Instead of using just one colour in the needle, mix different tones. Stranded cottons are available in ready-shaded colours, but provide only random tonal changes. To control the effect yourself, mix the colours as you work – versatile stranded cotton has six separate strands. Change the colour balance after each needleful – sooner if your design requires.

Mono canvas is the best choice, and the threads you use depend on the gauge of the canvas – any weight and combination as long as coverage is good. Cottons, silks, metallic threads and wools even with beads added, can work happily side by side, so go ahead and start mixing.

Below: On a detailed picture like this one, keep the main shapes simple. Use up thread oddments on a random border.

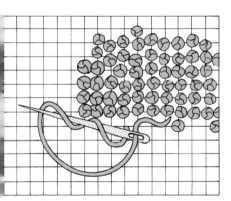

French knots

Bring the thread out where you want to make the knot, anchor it with a finger and wind the loose thread twice round the needle. Still holding the thread, re-insert the needle close to where the thread first emerged. Pull the thread through to the back.

black felt-tip pen. This makes the design easier to see through the canvas. Transfer the outlines to the canvas using the waterproof marker. Mark the position of the inner and outer borders shown in the positioning diagram by counting threads.

Mount the canvas on a frame large enough to accommodate the whole design. Once the canvas is fixed in place, do not remove it until the design is completed.

Stitching the freestyle picture

Work from the centre outwards. The design uses mainly stranded cotton. Use three strands of each colour, separating the strands as you need them to avoid tangles and help the stitches lie smoothly.

The centre square Begin with this area – sections A, B, C and D are all stitched in close French knots using mixed greens. Follow the same method for each section. In area A, there are five shades of green. Start with three strands of the first green in the needle. Scatter the French knots in the first area until the first needleful is finished. Then change to the second, third and fourth greens and drop the first one. Continue like this until the whole area is filled. Repeat for areas B, C and D using the colours shown in the picture.

Area M Work the sky area in the centre square using the shaded blue stranded cotton. This automatically produces an effect of 'clouds'. Work the random Gobelin filling stitch in patches, moving to a new patch when the thread colour changes. All the stitches should end in the same horizontal top row.

The main picture area Work the beautifully trimmed trees in random Byzantine stitch as described on the previous page. Fill in the main part of the sky (area K) using tent stitch. Try as far as possible to make the different colours link up with those in the centre square.

Add the two L areas in random Gobelin filling stitch, with the three strands of shaded thread, this time taken from different cut lengths so that they are mixed in the needle and form mottled areas.

The crazy paving First establish the dark grey tent stitch lines which run between each paving stone. Use the three lighter greys for the stones (random Gobelin filling stitch). Thread the needle with three strands of the first grey. Change the colour for each paving stone as for the central trees.

The border Stitch one row of jade green tent stitch all round the design, working into the same holes as the outer picture stitches. Next, work two rows of sloping satin stitch in wools, over three horizontal and three vertical threads. Stitch outer border in a completely free way, using a random mixture of stitches and colours. Those used here include French knots, slanted Gobelin stitch, straight stitches at any angle, cross stitch and oblong cross stitch. Sew on the pink and green beads at random using the crewel needle and one strand of stranded cotton.

Finishing off Check the whole picture for any missed stitches and take it off the frame. Stretch carefully and frame.

Stitch guide

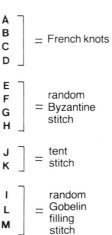

A B C D	= French knots
E F G H	= random Byzantine stitch
J K	= tent stitch
I L M	= random Gobelin filling stitch
	= mixed colours

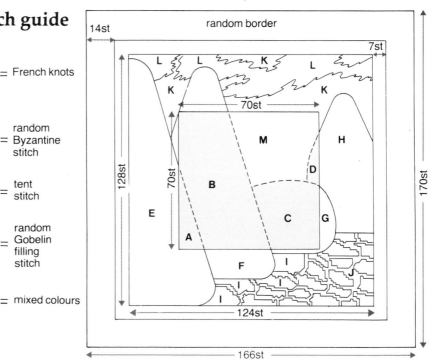

CHAPTER 10

A versatile alphabet for personalized stitchery

A decorative stitched alphabet can be used in many ways for personalized needlepoint. Stitch a single letter as a greetings card or mount it on a cushion. Two skip stitch backgrounds and a ribbon or flower border are given to frame the individual letters.

The charted letters are easy to work using continental tent stitch. Choose from two different border and background styles – you can frame the letter with matching ribbon and stitch a lacy background or work an open-textured background with a pretty floral border pattern. One vertical and one horizontal mounting is given.

These greetings cards with a difference will last for a long time – stitch the recipient's initial on canvas and mount with white or coloured card.

Letter with ribbon border

The satin ribbon border round the letter C is held in place with quick fishbone cross stitch. A skip stitch background to the letter gives a light, lacy effect. Use cotton threads for the whole design.

You will need

20cm/8in square piece of white 18-gauge mono canvas
2 skeins Twilleys embroidery stranded cotton in deep pink 517 *or* deep blue 639
1 skein in pale pink 522 *or* pale blue 641
1 ball DMC Cordonnet cotton No 3 in white
70cm/¾yd Offray single face satin ribbon in 156 Hot pink *or* 311 Blue mist (width 10mm/½in)
20cm/8in square stretcher bars or frame
Tapestry needle size 22
Chenille needle

Working the needlepoint

Use the full six strands of the stranded cotton throughout – strip the stranded cotton as described on page 35 – and a single strand of Cordonnet cotton over the ribbon border.
Find the centre of the canvas and, using a waterproof marker or pencil, mark a central rectangle 94 threads by 82 threads. This outline

marks the position of the solid deep pink line round the outside of the border. Work all letters in an upright frame, except M and W which are worked horizontally. If possible, mount the canvas on stretcher bars or a frame – the ribbon will be much easier to manage.

Stitch the chosen initial in the centre of the marked rectangle (find the letter centre by counting stitches in both directions on the chart) using continental tent stitch and following the chart colour key. One square on the chart represents one tent stitch.

Complete the tent stitch border working from the chart. Make a picot edge outside the border line by adding one stitch every four threads. Leave eight threads between the inner and outer bands of the border (to accommodate ribbon). The deep pink picot edge is repeated on the inside.

Adding the ribbon Cut the ribbon into four pieces the exact length of the sides so that they overlap at each corner (see dotted lines on chart). Hold the ribbon in place with your thumb (or put a small stitch in it).

Using a single strand of Cordonnet cotton, work fishbone cross stitch over the ribbon following the order given in the chart. Begin at the top left-hand corner. When you reach the next corner, turn the canvas so that you are beginning at another 'top left' in the same way.

The corners Using a sharp chenille needle and a single strand of Cordonnet cotton, work crossed corners over eight threads in each corner to anchor the ribbon thoroughly in place (piercing it in two places at each corner).

Background This is covered by a skip stitch – large-and-small cross stitch with every other stitch missed out. Begin in one corner to ensure that the pattern repeat fits exactly. Work large base cross stitches over four canvas threads, then cover with a small upright cross stitch over two threads, placing the horizontal stitch last on all stitches. The rest of the canvas is left unworked. When stitching close to the initial, shorten stitches where necessary, but be careful not to change the angle.

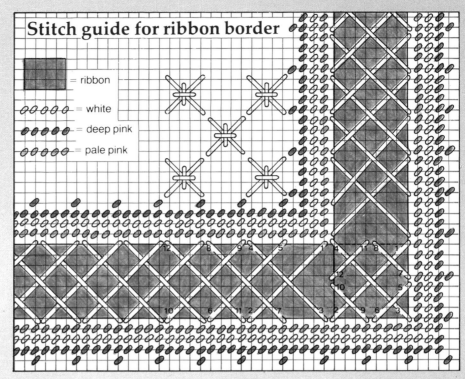

Stitch guide for ribbon border

= ribbon

= white

= deep pink

= pale pink

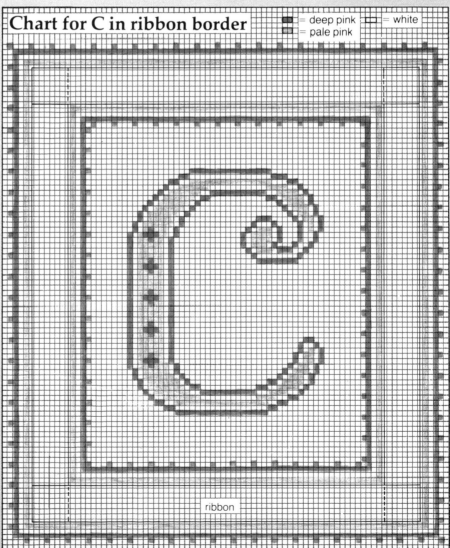

Chart for C in ribbon border

= deep pink   = white
= pale pink

ribbon

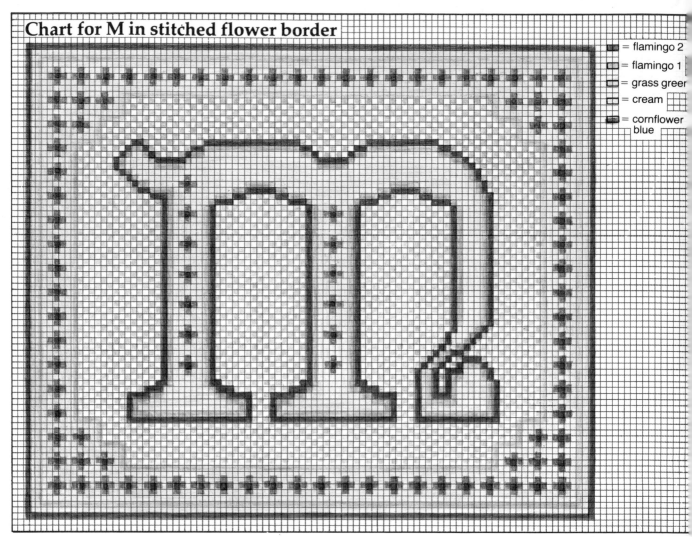

Chart for M in stitched flower border

= flamingo 2
= flamingo 1
= grass green
= cream
= cornflower blue

Letter with stitched flower border

The letter M shown as a horizontal greetings card has a pretty stitched flower border derived from the pattern on the alphabet letters. It is worked in a combination of crewel wool and stranded cotton in soft colours.

You will need
20cm/8in square piece of white 18-gauge mono canvas
Tapestry needle size 22
1 small skein each Appletons crewel wool in Cornflour Blue 4 (464), Grass Green 1 (251), Flamingo 1 and 3 (621 and 623)
3 skeins Twilleys embroidery stranded cotton in 843 (cream)
20cm/8in square frame (optional)

Working the needlepoint
Mark a rectangle in the centre of the canvas, 95 threads by 79 threads. Find the centre of the chosen letter by counting stitches horizontally and vertically on the chart. Stitch your letter in the centre of the marked rectangle using continental tent stitch and counting each stitch from the chart.

Use two strands of crewel wool for the coloured parts of the letter, and the full six strands of cream stranded cotton for the main filling. Finish off all threads carefully within the area of the letter so that there are no trailing threads across the background.

Work the border in continental tent stitch starting with the outer row of the frame in blue along the marked line of the rectangle. Continue with the cream and green border lines and lastly the flowers within the green border lines worked in pink with a central stitch in blue.

Background Lastly, fill in the area round the letter with skip tent stitch using one strand of pink crewel wool.

Skip tent stitch

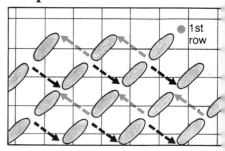

Working from right to left, begin at the dot on the diagram. Work a downward diagonal tent stitch. Miss out the next vertical canvas thread, and work another stitch on the next.

For the second row, work back from left to right so that your stitches form diagonal lines with those in the row above.

To keep the background light and lacy, use the border of the letter to anchor threads, and never start a row without enough thread in the needle to finish it.

Charts for letters

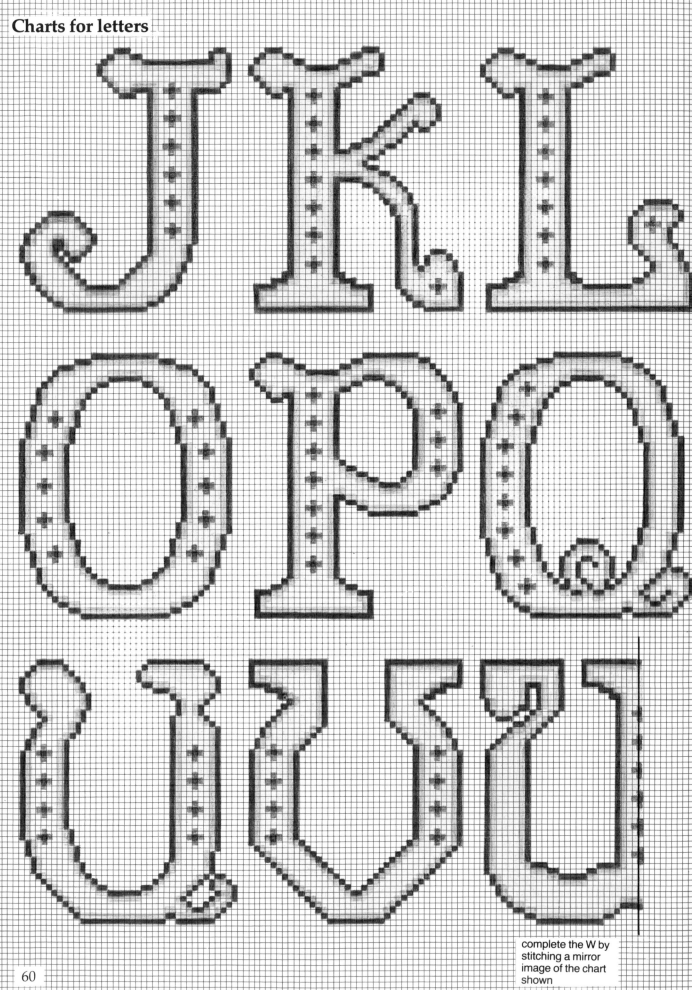

complete the W by
stitching a mirror
image of the chart
shown

1 square = 1 stitch

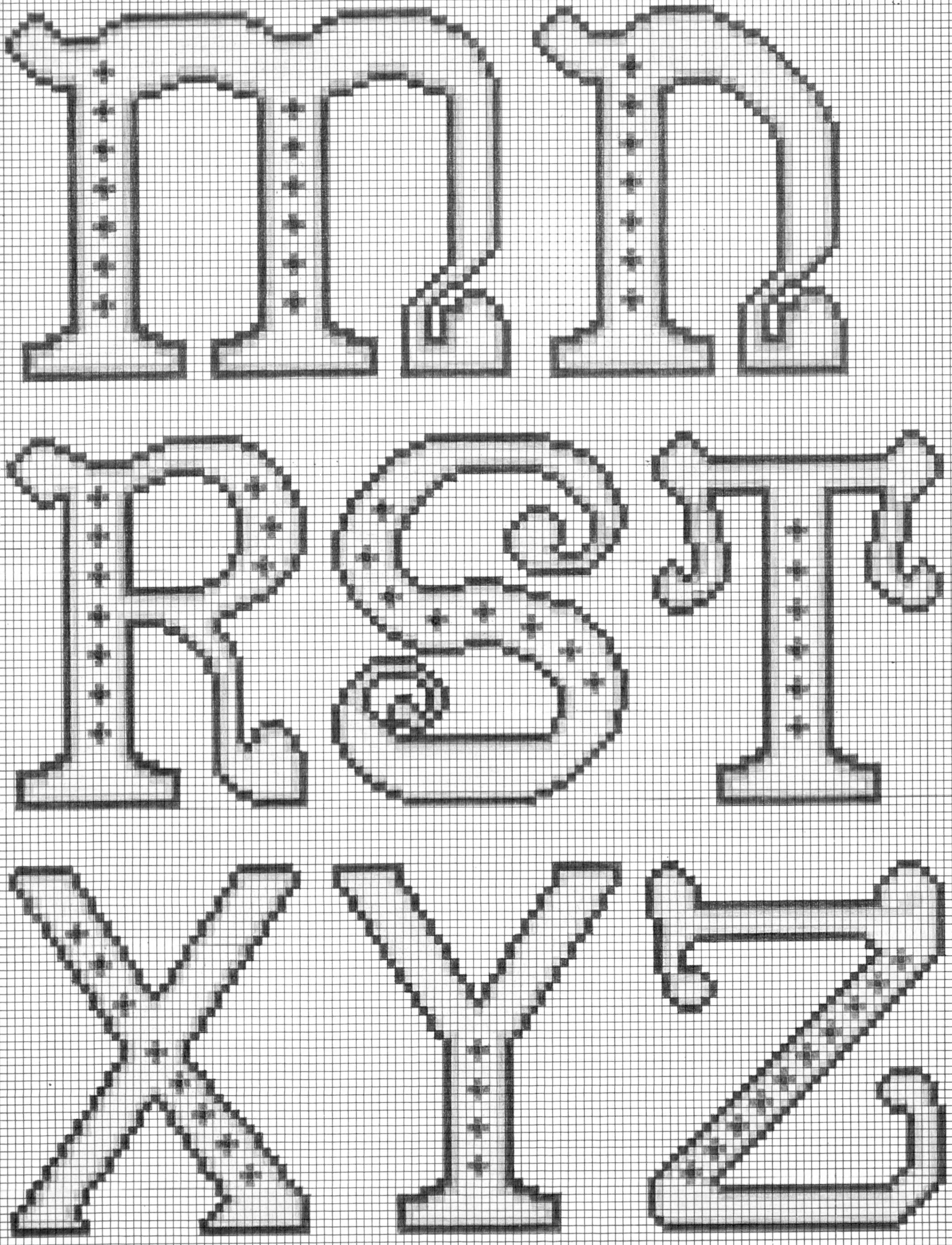

Cushions and cards with stitched initials

Use the needlepoint letters to make up a cushion or greetings card as a personalized gift. After stitching the canvas, block and set it carefully as described on page 23 before making it up so that the design forms a perfect rectangle.

Use masking tape to mount the initials in the card so that the needlepoint can be removed easily and preserved as a memento in a small frame. See page 27 for instructions on framing canvas. This attractive alphabet can also be used as a basis for larger projects. The cushion shown on page 68, for example, has a whole name as the main feature of the design. Alternatively, use the simple letters and numbers given in the chart below to sign and date your other canvas projects.

Right: A pair of small cushions with covers chosen to tone with the needlepoint. The blue one is made up as a herbal sleep pillow with the letter set in a window cut in the fabric. The broderie anglaise one has the letter appliquéd to the front.

Personalize a pretty cushion

Make someone a little cushion with their initial on it to decorate a bed or chair. Choose a cushion cover to match one of the colours in the needlepoint, or make one up yourself. Fill it with herbs or lavender for a fragrant sleep pillow.

Cushion with appliquéd letter Trim the canvas outside the needlepoint to 1cm/½in. Carefully remove the thread running along next to the stitching on all four sides. This makes it easier to fold the canvas back neatly. (Note: not possible with interlock canvas.) Trim off a small square at each corner, outside the thread you have just removed.

Fold the canvas over close to the stitching and tack the needlepoint on to the cushion cover front or cushion cover fabric, centring it carefully. Slipstitch it neatly, but firmly in place and remove tacking. Make up the cushion cover as normal if you're making your own.

Sleep pillow Leave the background to your letter unworked to allow the aroma through. Cut a window in the cushion front, neaten edges and apply needlepoint behind the opening.

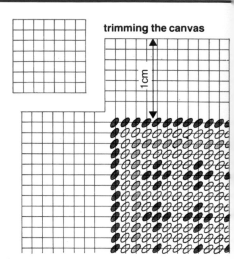

trimming the canvas

1cm

PROFESSIONAL TOUCH

Simple needlepoint letters and numbers

This plain and simple alphabet and numerals are invaluable for all kinds of needlepoint projects. They can be worked in continental tent stitch or cross stitch.

When you have put time and hard work into a beautiful piece of canvas work, it's certainly worth including your initials and/or the date in one corner.

Or you can stitch other people's names, initials or birthday dates on smaller projects – you could include them on a little tent stitch panel inserted in the bag or glasses case from chapter 5. Add your own initials to the centre square of the Renaissance Garden cushion in chapter 6 or sign the orchid design from chapter 2 in one corner.

Chart for numbers

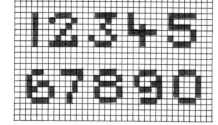

Chart for alphabet

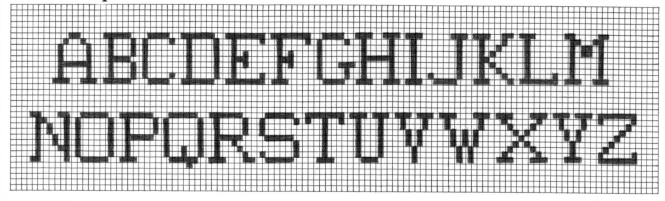

A personal greetings card

Send someone a stitched letter to celebrate birthdays, Christmas, christenings, or any special occasion. For perfect presentation, make one of these cards – they are far too good to throw away, and can be framed up as pictures, or the needlepoint removed and used to decorate any of the items suggested here.

You can easily obtain plain white and cream-coloured card; it also comes in a wide range of colours – choose one to tone with the needlepoint.

The pink and blue ribbon-bordered initials are perfect for a new baby and you could make a larger card and spell out the whole name instead of just the initial.

For an extra special Christmas card which can double as a small gift, how about stitching NÖEL in bright red and green threads and adding a border of red or green ribbon. You will, of course, need extra canvas.

You will need
Metal ruler and craft knife
Art card 20cm×54cm/8in×21in
Masking tape, width 2.5cm/1in
Adhesive for paper

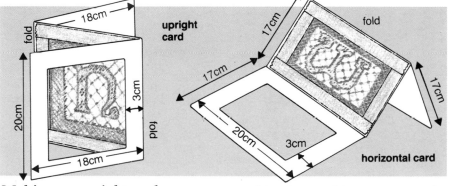

Making an upright card
Trim the canvas to within eight threads on all four sides.
For all letters except M and W, make an upright card. Divide the strip of card into three panels, each 18cm/7in wide. Mark these divisions accurately across the card and using the metal ruler and a *blunt* pointed instrument, score along the two lines, one on each side of the card so that the card bends easily into a zigzag shape. Mark and cut out a central rectangle from one of the end panels, leaving a 3cm/1¼in border all round.
Mount the canvas centrally on the middle panel behind this window. Secure along all four sides with

masking tape making sure none of the tape shows through the cut-out. Apply adhesive to the masking tape, fold the cut-out panel on top and stick in place as shown.

Making a horizontal card
For the letters M and W, trim the length of the card strip to 51cm/21in and divide it into three panels 17cm/7in wide. Cut out a rectangle, leaving a 3cm/1¼in border as before – this time mount the canvas sideways.
Finish the card as described above for vertical letters.
For names or words, use a horizontal card, adjusting size of needlepoint and mount as needed.

CHAPTER 11

Lacy pulled thread stitches

*With its open mesh and even weave, canvas makes an excellent ground fabric for pulled thread work.
The finished surface looks delicate, but is surprisingly tough. Much of the canvas is left showing,
so it's quick to work and gives a lovely pale effect.*

Eighteenth century white openwork embroidery of Germany and Denmark contains early examples of pulled thread work. It was called Dresden work or Dresden Point and originated as a time-saving alternative to real lace, often used for ladies' caps, fichus and aprons.

Pulled thread work should not be confused with drawn thread work, where threads are cut and completely removed from the ground fabric. In pulled thread, fabric threads are moved out of alignment by making different embroidery stitches and pulling these up tightly. This creates holes which form the pattern and give the work a delicate, lacy look.

Colour schemes

Traditionally, white thread on a white background was the rule. While you can use bold colour, it is usually more successful to make a soft combination of white, cream and beige with possibly a gentle accent of pale pink, green or blue. The reason for this is that the pattern is formed mainly by the *holes*; the thread only serves to bind the canvas threads together, so it should blend with the ground fabric as unobtrusively as possible.

For a project like a pulled thread cushion cover, mounting the worked canvas on a deep-coloured backing accentuates the pattern.

Materials

Canvas White mono canvas is the

Pulled thread stitch patterns for needlepoint

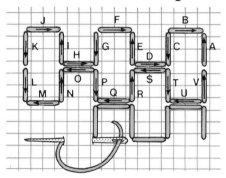

Honeycomb filling stitch

This pretty stitch leaves much of the canvas showing. Single vertical stitches and double horizontal ones create a honeycomb effect when pulled. Work all the stitches over three canvas threads.

Work from right to left on the first row. The letters indicate the order

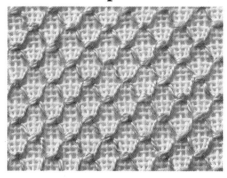

of holes in which to bring the needle up for each stitch.

On the second row, work back from left to right after taking a stitch into the surrounding canvas between the last stitch of the first row and first stitch of the second. Pulling the horizontal stitches tightly makes the pulled thread pattern.

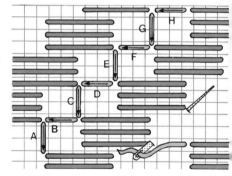

Blocks and single faggot pattern

Satin stitch blocks which are not pulled run between the diagonal lines of pulled stitches in a step pattern. The blocks are worked first, over six threads, the step pattern stitches next, over three. Use two different shades for the best effect.

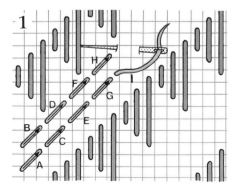

Diagonal chain and straight stitch

Pulled thread chain pattern is not related to regular chain stitch, on fabric or canvas.

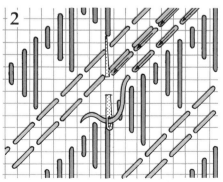

Here, little straight stitch triangles (not pulled) are used in diagonal rows between rows of the chain pattern.

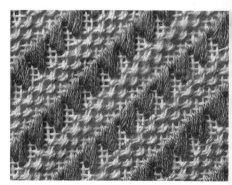

Follow diagram letters for the working order of the chain pattern as before, stitching two parallel rows at once.

only choice. Take care not to buy interlock canvas – the threads will not pull nicely.

Thread This must be strong enough to withstand constant pulling. Pearl cotton, crochet cotton, stranded cotton and fine string are all suitable. In general, the working thread should be the same thickness or finer than the canvas.

Stranded cotton should be stripped down as usual before use. Take care to align the thread plies when stitching, for a smooth finish.

Frames It is essential to use a frame for successful pulled thread work.

Needles It's a good idea to use a tapestry needle one size larger than that usually recommended for the canvas gauge. This helps to enlarge the decorative holes. Use the normal size of needle for non-pulled thread stitches; a fine, sharp needle is useful for finishing off threads in the back of the work.

Pulled thread techniques

Try to work any areas surrounding pulled thread stitchery first. This gives you a firm area to anchor the thread used for pulling the stitches. Make sure no loose threads trail across the back of an area to be pulled. If there are no surrounding stitches to anchor a new thread, leave an end about 6cm/2¼in long, running away from the work, and darn it into the back of the completed work later, using a sharp needle.

Following charts To obtain the correct 'pull' over a whole design, follow any working order instructions carefully. If, when starting a new line, you need to bring the needle up in the same hole as the last stitch finished, take a small stitch into the surrounding canvas, then return to the occupied hole.

Tension and pulling Everyone's tension varies and there's no right or wrong, but keep it constant and watch working charts for stitches that don't need to be pulled at all.

Pull upwards evenly on each stitch and ease the canvas threads together by pulling directly above where the needle will next go down through the canvas. Below the canvas, pull down evenly beneath the hole that is the up-point of the next stitch.

Below are some attractive patterns. Try creating your own effects combining pulled and regular stitches.

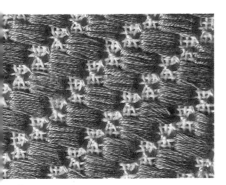

Working from right to left and upwards, begin at the lower right-hand corner of the stitching area with the first block of three stitches. The next block is positioned three horizontal threads higher than the first. Turn and work the pulled stitches in the order indicated.

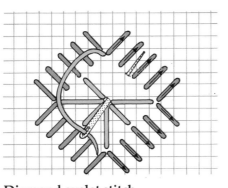

Diamond eyelet stitch
This example shows the diamond eyelets in a framework of diagonal overcast stitches worked in a different shade of thread.
Work the diagonal overcast stitches first, in zigzag rows from left to right, then from right to left, to create the diamond-shaped spaces.

Then add the diamond-shaped eyelets using eight stitches for each one, worked into the same central hole.

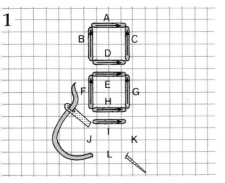

Four-sided stitch
1 Work each stitch over three threads, forming a design of squares which makes an attractive

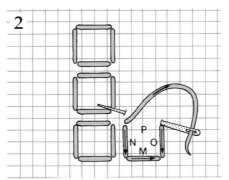

pattern when stitches are pulled.
2 Work in vertical rows in the order shown in the diagram. The letters indicate where to bring the needle

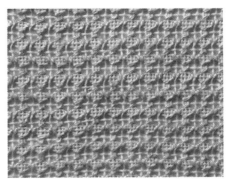

up for each stitch and the arrows show the direction of the stitch.
A series of large cross stitches forms on the back of the work.

65

A pretty mirror frame

Gluing a square of worked canvas over an ordinary mirror tile makes an attractive piece of needlepoint to hang on the wall. The cut-out centre of the canvas shows the mirror which also glints behind the holes in the pulled thread work, accentuating the lacy look. Toning ribbons secured with oblong cross stitch make a pretty frame for the squares.

You will need
30cm/12in square mirror tile
40cm/16in square 18-gauge mono white canvas
4m/4⅜yd satin ribbon, width 10mm/⅜in, in coffee colour
4 skeins DMC stranded cotton in fawn (543)
2 skeins DMC pearl cotton No 5 in salmon (948), 1 skein in ecru
2 small skeins Appleton's crewel wool in Flame Red 3 (203)
1 ball DMC Cotonia (a soft knitting cotton) in shade 2429 (cream)
Stretcher bars or frame

Tapestry needles size 20 and 22
Fine, sharp needle

Marking the canvas
Using the chart (below) mark the square of canvas with the positions for the ribbon and cross stitch borders framework. (When working the design these should be stitched first and the other stitches – shown in detail earlier – filled in afterwards). Mark in the lines with a pencil on lines of *holes*, not threads. **Note:** one square on the chart represents *two* canvas threads. The ribbon and cross stitch bands span eight threads so that they are four squares wide on the chart. The padded cross stitch borders on either side of the bands cover two threads and the pattern squares each span 36 threads in either direction.

Right: If you prefer to make a cushion, work the centre square area as well.

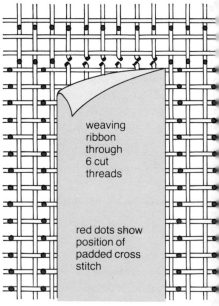

Chart for mirror frame

1 square = 2 threads

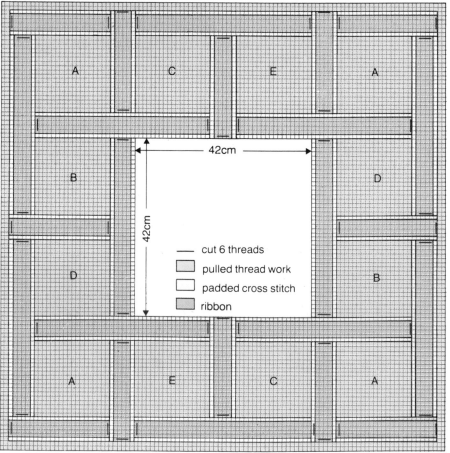

42cm

42cm

— cut 6 threads
▨ pulled thread work
☐ padded cross stitch
▨ ribbon

Working the needlepoint

weaving ribbon through 6 cut threads

red dots show position of padded cross stitch

The ribbon framework
Having pencilled in placement lines, make slits in the canvas where indicated, in order to pass lengths of ribbon through to the back of the canvas. With a pair of small, sharp scissors, carefully snip through six threads in the centre of the eight-thread band at the points marked on the chart.

from the ribbon, cut eight 35cm/
14in lengths and four 10cm/4in
lengths. Keeping the canvas and
ribbon flat, weave the ribbon into
place, following the over and under
pattern, see chart, pushing one
ribbon through to the back every
time two ribbons cross, to avoid a
double thickness.

Padded cross stitch
When the ribbons are all in place,
work round all edges of each piece
(except where ribbons finish at
outer edge of design) using padded
cross stitch. Use three strands of
crewel wool for the straight
padding and three strands of the
stranded cotton for the cross
stitch on top. Pierce the ribbon
where necessary to hold it in place.
On back of canvas, trim ribbons and
stick ends to canvas.

Completing the framework
Now work oblong cross stitch
across each section of ribbon
using the soft knitting cotton and
making the stitches over four
vertical and eight horizontal canvas
threads.

Work a border of crossed corners
round the outside of the whole
design using one strand of the ivory
pearl cotton.

Working the panels
All the stitch patterns you need are
described in this chapter.
Begin with the four corner squares
(A) which are worked in diamond
eyelet stitch in a diagonal overcast
stitch framework. Use six strands of
stranded cotton for the overcast
stitches and one strand salmon
pearl cotton for the eyelets, going
round each eyelet twice.
Stitch the panels marked B using
four-sided stitch over three threads.
Use one strand of salmon pearl
cotton.
Next work the panels marked C in
the diagonal chain and straight
stitch pattern. Use six strands of the
stranded cotton for the triangles
and do not pull the stitches. Then,
using one strand of salmon pearl
cotton, work the pulled diagonal
chain stitch.
Use blocks and single faggot pattern
for the two panels marked D. Use
six strands of the stranded cotton

for the upright satin stitches and
one strand of salmon pearl cotton
for the pulled single faggot stitch.
Finally, fill the two panels marked E
with honeycomb filling stitch using
one strand of salmon pearl cotton.

Making up
Take the worked canvas off the
frame and cut out the central
unworked area to within five
threads of the inner cross stitch.
Now turn back the canvas all
round, close to the cross stitch and
snipping diagonal cuts at the
corners, being careful not to snip
the threads holding the cross stitch.
Glue the canvas back behind the
ribbon border.
On outside edge, trim canvas back
to within eight threads of edge. On
all sides, remove the canvas thread
immediately adjacent to the outer
worked edge (this helps the canvas
to fold more easily) and trim
corners. Fold excess canvas to the
back and glue lightly. Finger-press.
Now glue canvas over mirror tile –
outer edges should be flush.
Fix on the wall using the adhesive
pads supplied.

CHAPTER 12

Simple straight stitches form Florentine wave patterns

Florentine stitchery forms striking zigzag patterns. The tradition goes back a long way, particularly for soft furnishings, and it's satisfyingly quick to do. Patterns are built up from a basic pattern row – start by following these charts and you'll soon be designing your own.

The dramatic and attractive effect of Florentine stitches, and the simplicity and speed of working them has probably done more than anything else to make needlepoint so popular. Florentine embroidery has several other names – among them, Bargello, Hungarian point, Flame stitch and Irish stitch. Its origins are rather obscure, but it was certainly popular on both sides of the Atlantic in the 18th century where it was worked in wools for upholstered wing chairs, and in silks for small items such as purses and belts.

What is Florentine stitchery?

Traditionally, Florentine stitch is a series of upright stitches, worked in repeating patterns. In its most basic form it covers four canvas threads with a jump up (or down) of two horizontal threads between each stitch, making a zigzag effect of alternate peaks and valleys. Countless variations are made by altering the stitch length, the size of the jump up or down, or by working two or more parallel stitches. The two most important characteristics of any design are its pattern repeat and its colours.

Florentine patterns

There are several easily recognisable types of Florentine design. Charts for some simple wave patterns are shown right. Once the basic row is established on the canvas, it is often just a matter of progressing down the canvas, copying the pattern underneath it in the chosen colours.

Florentine stitch The most basic wave pattern is the traditional Florentine stitch itself. The peaks and valleys are all the same depth, so the stitch forms an even zigzag. The yarn colour is usually changed with every row.

Deep wave stitch By making some of the stitches longer, or increasing the step height (jump between stitches) deeper pattern rows can be planned. These patterns look best worked over larger canvas areas – cushions, carpets and chair or stool covers. If the area is not deep enough, the design cannot be developed fully, so choose patterns carefully. With simple, shallow patterns, you can stitch smaller and narrower items such as belts.

Rounded patterns Curves can be introduced into classic Florentine

needlepoint seat cover

lattice pattern

unusual wave pattern

flame pattern

Chart for simple wave patterns

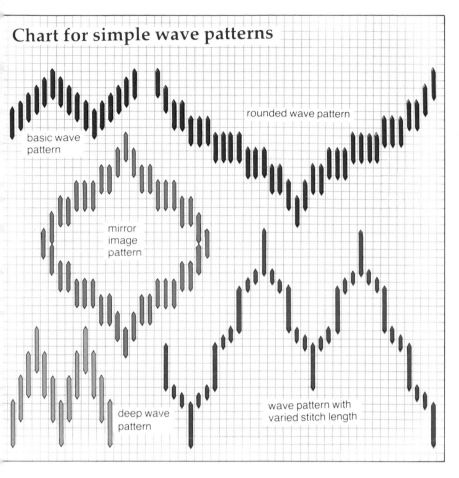

basic wave pattern

rounded wave pattern

mirror image pattern

deep wave pattern

wave pattern with varied stitch length

flame patterns by working blocks of stitches of the same height next to each other. The step height between blocks or between a block and a stitch determines whether the curves are gentle or sharp.

Mirror image patterns By repeating a pattern upside down underneath itself, a mirror image pattern is formed. These patterns form rows of symmetrical motifs such as diamonds, or curved onion shapes. The new spaces which may appear between these motifs need to be filled.

Working techniques

Mono (single thread) canvas is the most suitable for Florentine work. Work into each vertical row of holes, and make each stitch in two movements. The stitches should share holes with the ones above and below. Canvas coverage is most important. Remember that straight stitches do not cover the canvas as well as diagonal ones, so you may need extra strands of yarn, or a finer canvas than you normally use for tent stitch with a particular yarn. Always test the stitch and yarn first to check coverage.

mirror image medallion pattern

classic rounded wave pattern

garland pattern

four-way design of repeated hearts

four-way heart design contrasting shades

four-way design in toning shades

Florentine pattern charts are usually given as grids where each square represents one canvas hole. Begin by working a complete pattern row or repeat from the chart. Take great care to stitch accurately, taking note of the length of each stitch and the step height between stitches.

Colour planning

Florentine designs provide an opportunity to create stunning colour effects. Traditionally the patterns are worked in subtle tonal gradation, the colours shading from light into dark and back. Two, or perhaps three basic colours are combined – each represented by several different tones. Nowadays, bolder colour combinations are also seen – several unrelated colours in the same design can look effective.

The interaction of neighbouring colours is important – closely related colours like green and blue blend quietly together, whereas more distant colours like red and blue look

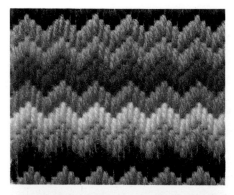

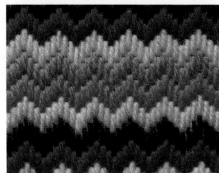

Above: The jazzier contrasting effect.
Top: The calm and harmonious effect.

much jazzier. The wide colour range of embroidery yarns means that you can stitch magnificently-shaded designs and even the simplest wave repeat can look sophisticated in subtle shades.

By changing the order of colours, the same design can be given a completely different look, using exactly the same shades. To experiment, take two shades of brown, two of coral, and white. For a calm and harmonious effect work a simple wave pattern in the order: light brown, dark brown, light brown, white, light coral, dark coral, light coral, light brown, dark brown, etc.

Now work the same pattern in white, dark coral, dark brown, white, light coral, light brown, white, dark coral, dark brown, etc. This jazzy effect is much more contemporary and the colours 'jostle' with each other more. This is because a higher proportion of white is used and because the stronger colours are not next to their own lighter tones.

Florentine belt

Here's a pretty Florentine belt. The very simple zigzag pattern is worked as a mirror image to give a row of diamonds in the centre.

You will need

For a belt up to 76cm/30in waist:
Piece of 18-gauge mono canvas (white), canvas width×15cm/6in
Small skeins of Appleton's crewel wool: 1×Bright rose 6; 3×Royal blue 1; 3×Scarlet 1; 2×Leaf 6; 2×Bright China 7; 2×Fuschia 4
Tapestry needle size 22
Metal belt clasp
10cm/4in moiré or acetate backing fabric
Masking tape

Stitching the belt

Measure the depth of the shank of your chosen belt clasp – the width of the finished belt depends on this. The belt in the picture has a shank size of 5cm/2in. To make a wider belt, work extra pattern rows or, if the increase is slight, work on a slightly coarser canvas – check that the thread still covers the different gauge of canvas and if not use a thicker thread.

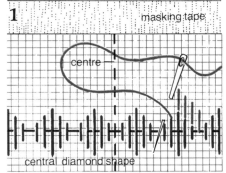

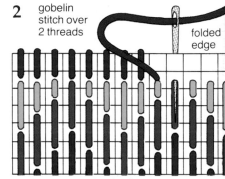

1 Bind the piece of canvas.
Stitch the simple zigzag design from chart, using three strands of crewel wool and beginning at the centre of the canvas. Start with the central diamond shapes – each one is worked over two, four, six, four and two threads. Then stitch the rows of zigzags over three threads and fill in with the triangles to make a straight edge.

2 When the exact waist measurement is reached, bend the unworked canvas over along both long edges, leaving two threads on the right side, next to the stitched area. Pinch this turning well with your fingers. Work a row of straight gobelin stitch over the two threads along both sides of the belt. Stitch through both thicknesses of canvas, aligning the holes as you work.

Making up the belt

Trim the short ends of the canvas to 2cm/¾in. Turn under and catch stitch.

3 Turn in the long edges of the backing fabric. Using a small, sharp needle, stitch backing to the needlepoint along all edges, having the fabric extending 5cm/2in at each end. Thread the extended backing fabric through the clasp at both ends, trim and stitch in place. This avoids damaging the needlepoint by having it constantly pulling against the metal.

Chart for belt

Appletons crewel wool shade nos.

▬ = 946	▬ = 426
▭ = 821	▬ = 747
▬ = 501	▬ = 804

Using Florentine stitch patterns

Use the chart for simple wave patterns to experiment with different colour combinations and, at the same time, make a variety of useful and colourful needlepoint items for your wardrobe and home.

A single mirror repeat along a length of canvas can make a strong and practical shoulder strap for a favourite bag. Double the mirror repeat for extra depth to make a belt to fit a wider fastening.

Parallel bands of deep wave pattern can build up graded tones of colour for a cushion cover. Use a medium gauge canvas and crewel or tapestry wools for this greater area.

Pick out one or two colours from a pair of curtains to make some simple tie backs using the rounded patterns for extra depth.

The method for backing and finishing off given for the Florentine belt can be adapted for all these projects.

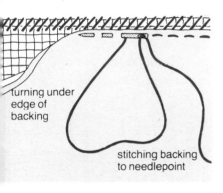

turning under edge of backing

stitching backing to needlepoint

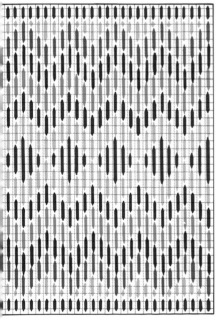

Above: These bright colours create an ethnic effect. The more muted colourway (right) shows a more traditional alternative.

CHAPTER 13

Planning a Florentine design

*Try working out pattern repeats and pretty four-way designs
using simple wave, mirror image and
medallion patterns and use variations in scale to fit these
patterns to a pre-determined shape. Stitch
a stunning shaped cummerbund using this technique.*

Planning a whole design depends on the shape and size of the project as well as on your chosen pattern. The Florentine sampler picture below shows you how several different kinds of design – all-over, linear or single motif patterns – can be planned to fit in a definite area, and at the same time, how well they can work together.

Different patterns, same shape

Adapting a favourite pattern to an item you are making is much easier than you might think. To understand how patterns fit into areas, take a basic shape such as a rectangle. This could be made into a long stool cover, a glasses case, a matchbox cover, a cheque book cover or an evening bag – objects of differing scales.

All-over patterns with small repeats are useful and will fill any shape easily – the exact final size of many items is not critical, so begin at the centre and work outwards, balancing pattern repeats until the whole area is filled. A good example

of this is trellis pattern. With all straight-edged items, work compensation stitches when you reach the top and lower edges to make them straight, maintaining pattern on inner ends of stitches.

Basic wave or mirror image designs can be planned for this shape in various ways. Obviously, the larger the project, the more stitches there will be in each pattern repeat (for added width) and the more horizontal rows there will be (for added height).

Uneven numbers of repeats seem to make for the most interesting designs – three, five or seven

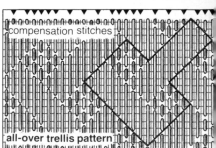

'peaks'. If your calculations suggest an even number will fit best, try to split the last motif in half to give an odd number of whole peaks with a half at either end. Whether working a mirror image or simple wave baseline, always establish the centre pattern lines on the canvas first.

Same pattern, different shapes

The diagram (right) shows how the same design – in this case a single or repeated medallion motif can be used to fit different basic shapes like squares and rectangles. A motif like this appears in the Florentine sampler. Although its height measures slightly more than its width, this is a design that will easily adapt to a square.

Taking the idea a step further, some designs can decide the shape of the project for you – for example the shaped cummerbund overleaf. The outline of the belt front follows the mirror-image pattern – curves are kept gentle by using blocks of same-length stitches (see below).

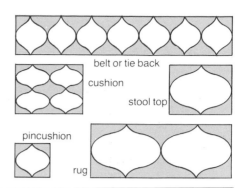

belt or tie back
cushion
stool top
pincushion
rug

Charting a pattern repeat

If you've already decided how many peaks you want across the design, divide the number of vertical canvas threads by this number to find the width of each peak and enable you to work out a pattern repeat. Do this in chart form, on a piece of graph paper. Remember that high and low pivot stitches on a pattern repeat must only be counted once.

If the height of the pattern needs to fit the item exactly (for instance the mirror-image band placed vertically in the sampler) take this into account, otherwise make as deep or shallow pattern as you wish, and work as many pattern rows in your chosen colour sequence as necessary to fill the area.

Left: All-over flame pattern (top left), single medallion motif with tent stitch surround (top centre), mirror-image wave border used vertically (right), single motif ribbon border with straight stitch background (centre), four-way rose motif (bottom left), all-over trellis pattern (bottom centre), initials in a pair of mirror-image medallions (bottom right).

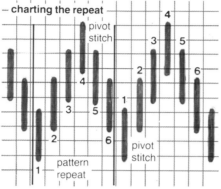

– charting the repeat –
pivot stitch
pattern repeat
pivot stitch

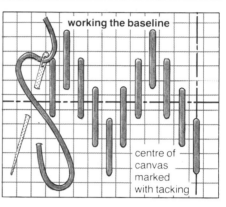

working the baseline
centre of canvas marked with tacking

Working the pattern baseline
Make an accurate paper template of the area to be worked. Lay this on the canvas and mark the area with a pencil. Cut out, leaving a good border. Count horizontal and vertical threads and mark the canvas centre. Always begin stitching at the centre.

Curves The more same-length stitches worked together in a pattern repeat, the flatter will be the curve and the wider the repeat. To increase width without affecting height, include some larger groups of same-length stitches and increase their height in small increments. For a smooth curve, increase stitch

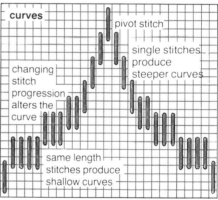

curves
changing stitch progression alters the curve
pivot stitch
single stitches produce steeper curves
same length stitches produce shallow curves

lengths in mathematical progressions such as 1, 2, 3 threads, 1, 3, 5, 7 threads, never in unrelated jumps such as 7, 2, 10, 4 threads.

Four-way Florentine patterns

An example of this appears at the bottom left of the sampler. These beautiful designs are based on a square divided diagonally into repeated quarters, the straight stitches lying in four different directions, radiating outwards from the centre hole.

Begin working at the centre. If necessary, you can stop wherever you like to fit an area exactly, although you should be able to determine this by counting threads. Mark the canvas centre and divide it diagonally in four with lines of tacking. Adjoining design repeats must share holes along these lines.

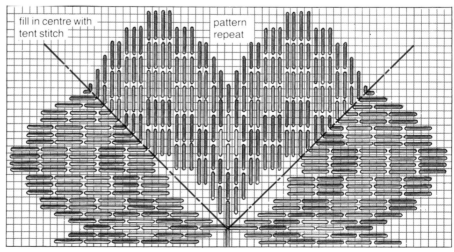

fill in centre with tent stitch
pattern repeat

Dazzling evening cummerbund

Above: Quick to stitch, this cummerbund makes a very versatile evening accessory

This wide cummerbund with its eye-catching combination of glowing colours framed in black and given a sparkle with gold embroidery thread, will be a stunning addition to evening outfits. The mirror-image Florentine design is based on rounded pattern lines.

You will need
Piece of 14-gauge mono canvas (canvas width ×20cm/8in)
1 skein each Paterna Persian yarn in pale emerald (501), dark emerald (500), magenta (645), blue (763)
8 skeins black (050)
5 reels Balger gold embroidery thread
Tapestry needle size 20

For making up
2m/2yd black bias binding
20cm/¼yd backing (plastic furnishing fabric such as Lionella)
4 large black hooks and eyes

Stitching the belt
First measure your waist accurately for a comfortable fit. The belt shown here fits a 71cm/28in waist. It has three of the lozenge motifs (marked D on the diagram) at each end. To enlarge or reduce the size, add or omit as many D motifs as necessary to obtain the nearest measurement *below* the waist measurement. (The width of each D motif is 6.5cm/2½in.) Continue the pattern symmetrically at each end of the belt until the waist measurement is reached.

Most of the stitches in the design are worked over four threads. Some of the gold stitches are worked over two.

Begin at the centre front of the belt – see chart – with three strands of the black yarn in the needle. Work the framework of black stitches first. Now fill in the green, blue and magenta stitches. Finally, add the gold stitches, using two thicknesses of the gold thread.

Fill in the area between the Florentine stitches and the edge of the belt as shown on the chart with diagonal tent stitch in black, using two strands of yarn.

Making up the belt

With brightly coloured tacking thread, tack round the edge of the belt. Place the tacking line between the second and third rows of tent stitch from the edge of the straight part of the belt and along the top of the long black stitches on the curved parts.

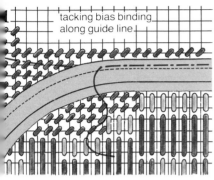

tacking bias binding along guide line

Using this line as a guide, tack the edge of the bias binding (along fold) to the belt, right sides together.
Wrong sides together, pin canvas centrally into position on piece of backing. Machine stitch along the tacked line through binding, canvas and backing fabric.

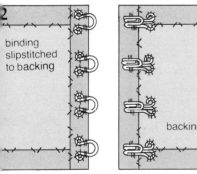

binding slipstitched to backing

backing

Remove tacking and trim canvas so there is one free thread lying between the needlepoint and the edge, with backing flush. Fold bias binding to inside of belt and slipstitch in place.
Bind the ends in the same way and attach the four hooks and eyes to close.

positioning guide for Florentine belt motifs

D D D C B C A C B C C C B C D D D

centre

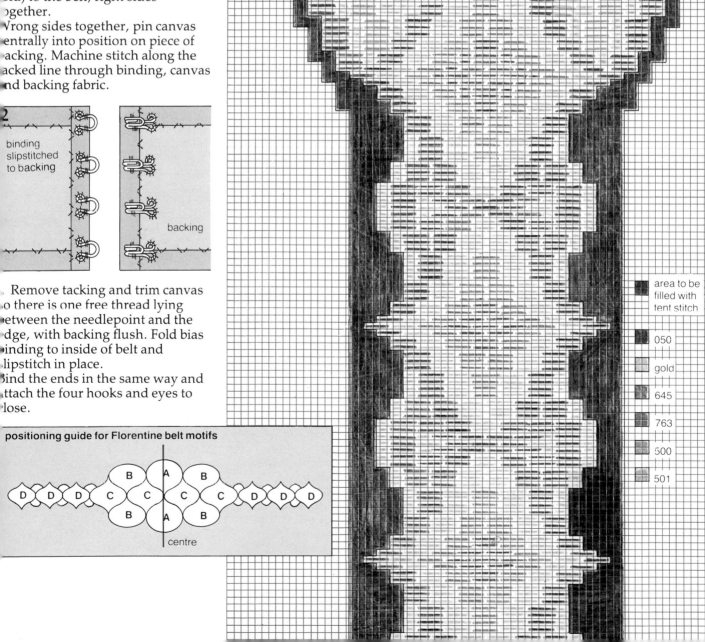

centre

area to be filled with tent stitch

050

gold

645

763

500

501

CHAPTER 14

Borders, corners and frames for Florentine needlepoint

Many needlepoint pieces benefit from having a stitched border. A border helps to link different colours in the main area and gives it a firm edge. Here's a choice of attractive borders to suit all kinds of design. Use one to stitch a photograph frame.

Needlepoint borders can be richly-coloured and intricately designed like the ones used on old Persian carpets. They may include several stitches. Often, however, all that's needed is the narrowest band of straight gobelin stitch or a few rows of tent stitch. Between these two extremes there are countless possibilities – learn how to choose the right one for your piece of work.

Types of border

Geometric borders are equally effective on geometric or pictorial needlepoint. A lattice border on a half cross stitch floral design is a good example (see cushion, page 15). An effective trick with designs like this is to stitch part of the main picture so that it breaks out of the frame, actually

overlapping it. This gives a three-dimensional feel.

A randomly-stitched border also works well on a picture (see page 54). You can make a pretty border from a repeated motif like hearts (see page 84). Florentine designs, too, make lovely borders (see page 72) and they're highly adaptable.

Borders can be used on their own as a straight band for items like belts and curtain tie-backs. Generally, any design will do provided it can be adapted to the required depth.

Frames Projects like mirror, picture and photograph frames, consist of the worked border on its own. This is a chance to use some of the more ornate borders. It is important to choose a design which turns corners happily.

Planning a border

Some borders will fit any size of design, others need careful counting of threads to make them fit. You may need to add stitches to the outer edge of the main design to match up the thread count with the border. With a geometric design in the centre, it's likely to be easier to adapt the border. Always mark the centre of the canvas before beginning to stitch, extending both tacking rows to the edge of the canvas. This means you have the centre of each side marked – important for border patterns which reverse in the centre or for repeated motif designs.

Borders with an exact thread count need more careful planning. Even with rows of a comparatively simple stitch such as crossed corners, the length of each side of the border must be a multiple of four threads – the number of threads spanned by each stitch – so an exact number of stitches can be fitted. Adjust the central design accordingly.

For a picture, it's a good idea to stitch the border after the main part of the design but *before* the background is worked. This means you can make alterations to your border plan when you see the effect of the pictorial design. Then you can work the all-over background in the spaces between the design and the border.

Borders to fit any size of design

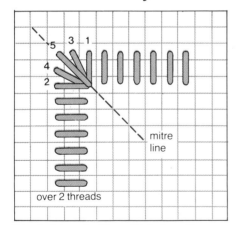

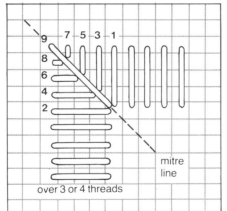

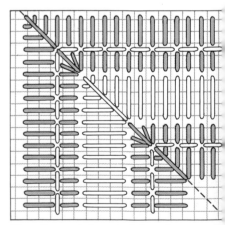

Straight gobelin stitch borders
This is a very useful stitch and adaptable to any size of border. When turning a corner with this stitch, you need to work in a slightly different way, depending on the number of threads you are working over.
Over two threads In this case, note

that you should stitch into the inner corner hole five times.
Follow working order on chart.
Over three or four threads Work each stitch into the diagonal mitre line of holes, the outermost ones being over one thread, then work a long stitch from inner to outer corner, to cover the ends.

Simple straight stitch border
Pick out one of the deeper colours in the central design for the outer and inner rows of straight gobelin stitch. Fill in the border area with more rows, varying the width of the bands.
Backstitch in pearl cotton between some of the rows looks very pretty.

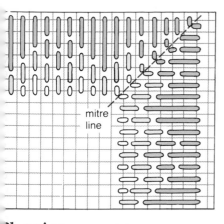

Planning a corner

The best way to deal with most border corners is to pencil a diagonal mitre line from the inner border corner to the outer. The border design should 'change direction' along this line, with stitches being worked into the holes along the line, keeping to the pattern as far as possible, shortening stitches where necessary. Patterns such as square motifs, do not need a mitre line – they fit naturally into the angle of the corner. This is clearly shown in the cushion stitch example (below right). Other ideas for corner squares are blocks of chequer stitch or a Florentine medallion.

Right: Use one of the borders in this chapter to stitch a pretty frame with a hanging ring or a standing support.

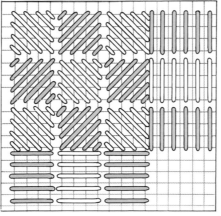

Cushion stitch striped border

Cushion stitch makes an ideal corner decoration on a straight gobelin stitch border. Use two different colours to make the diagonal stitch pattern show up. You could also work a block of cushion stitch at the centre of each side of a rectangular border.

Borders that can reverse in the centre

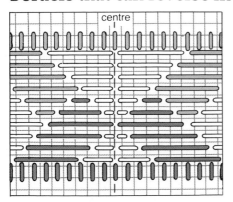

Plait border

This pretty border pattern must be worked in three colours to emphasize the plait effect.
It is worked entirely in straight horizontal or vertical stitches with an edging of straight gobelin stitch. Make it wider if you wish.
Reverse the pattern along the centre marked line of each side and follow the photograph to see how to treat the corner.

Borders that need to be counted

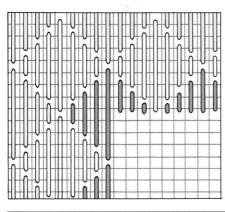

2, 4, 6, 8 stitch border

This diamond pattern fits well as long as each border side is a multiple of eight threads. Try working some of the 2, 4, 6, 8 stitches horizontally.
To adjust the measurement of the central design, add a row of cross stitch or straight gobelin stitch round the edge. If you add a row of straight gobelin over two threads, you have added four threads overall.

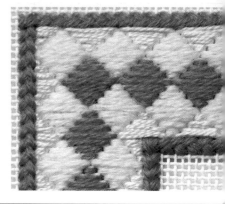

Ribbon border photograph frames

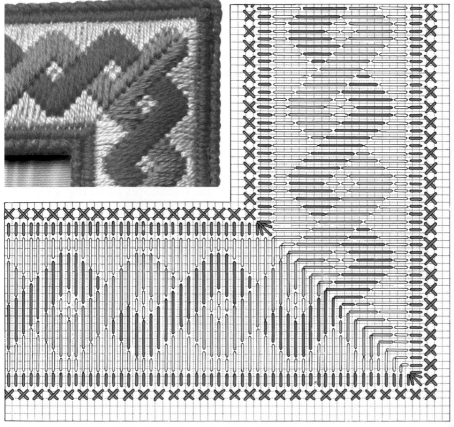

follow chart for bottom right and top left corners; follow inset for other two corners

These professional-looking photo graph frames are quick to stitch usin a pretty Florentine ribbon border.

You will need
For a frame 18cm×21cm/7in×8¼in (picture area 8cm×11.5cm/ 3¼in×4½in)
Piece of 14-gauge mono canvas 28cm×31cm/11in×12in
3×4g skeins Appleton's crewel wool in Flamingo 3 (623) and 3 skeins in Grey Green 1 (351)
2 skeins DMC pearl cotton No 5 in ivory (948)
2 tapestry needles size 20
For making up
Stiff card
Fabric adhesive
Oddment of lining fabric or moiré
For a frame 21cm×25.5cm/ 8¼in×10in (picture area 12cm×15.5cm/4¾in×6¼in)
Piece of 14-gauge mono canvas 31cm×36cm/12in×14in
1×25g/1oz hank Appleton's crewel wool in Flamingo 3 (623)
All other requirements as given for the smaller size frame.

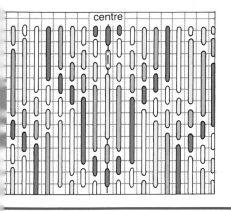

Gothic Florentine border

This spectacular border adapts well to any size. Begin on the centre line of one of the sides with a straight stitch over six threads, having one end at the border edge.

Work the design outwards on both sides of this central stitch, following the chosen colour sequence and reversing pattern on either side.

At corners, work stitches into the mitre line, shortening them where necessary.

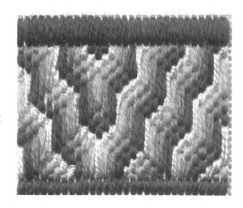

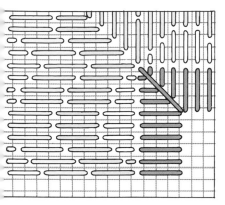

Double wave border

This Florentine-type border also has an eight-thread pattern repeat, the pivot stitch being counted once only (see page 73).

To stitch this border to a particular width, add extra row of the Florentine design, or build up with straight gobelin stitch, here used on either side of the pattern, over four threads.

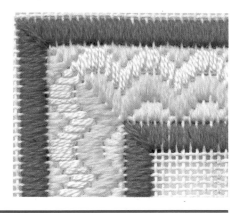

Stitching the frame

Mark the centre of the piece of canvas. Roughly mark out the central picture area of the frame (size as given in You will need, left) placing it centrally.

Work the ribbon pattern and the mitred corners from the chart. Use four strands each of the coral and green wools in the needle. It is easier to have one needle for each colour and work a little in each at a time.

Leave two free canvas threads outside the ribbon band and work straight gobelin stitch over two threads either side of them, using four strands of the coral wool. Add a row of cross stitch outside of these lines, using three strands.

Work the background to the ribbon pattern in satin stitch using two strands of the ivory pearl cotton.

Making up the frame

Cut two pieces of stiff card to the finished size of the frame you are making. Using a ruler, mark and cut out the central picture area

appropriate to the size, from one of the card rectangles.

Cut two pieces of the backing fabric to the size of the whole rectangle, plus 1.5cm/⅝in for seams. With right sides together, machine round two long sides and one short. Trim seams and corners and turn to right side. Press seams under on remaining short raw edges, insert uncut card rectangle and slipstitch edges closed. This is the back of the frame.

Make a fabric loop, insert through hanging ring, and stitch both ends to upper edge of frame back.

Take the worked canvas and machine all round inner and outer edges of border, close to the needlepoint using the closest shade of thread possible. Make slits in the canvas as shown, trim inner and outer canvas rebates to 1cm/½in. Make diagonal cuts at outer corners. Stick needlepoint to card frame, pull rebates to the back, and lace opposite edges tightly with strong thread.

Apply fabric glue carefully to front

side and lower edges of frame back. Stick needlepoint border portion carefully in place. Photographs can be inserted between the two layers at the top.

For a frame with a standing support, omit the hanging ring and cover a blunt-ended wedge shape of card with fabric, securing with fabric adhesive. Leave a small tongue of free fabric (at the narrower end of the wedge) and stick this to the back of the frame so that it is supported at the correct angle.

making up the frame

slits at inner and outer corners

CHAPTER 15

Using Florentine needlepoint for upholstered furniture

Hardwearing needlepoint is an ideal covering for upholstered furniture and Florentine patterns have been traditionally used for seats and stools. Learn how to stitch and cover a drop-in seat and experiment with medallion patterns to make up your own designs.

Upholstered pieces of furniture undergo considerable wear and tear and the materials used must be chosen accordingly. Wool yarns wear better than any others.

Do not choose too large a gauge of canvas or a pattern with very long stitches. A stitch worked over six threads of 10-gauge canvas will be almost twice as long as the same stitch on 18-gauge canvas, and twice as likely to fluff up and catch. As a guide, try not to use stitches worked over more than six threads and work on canvas no coarser than 14-gauge.

Choosing patterns

The scale of the pattern must complement the size of the piece – don't choose a very large pattern repeat for a small item. Rules are made to be broken, however, and a single bold Florentine motif can look stunning on a round stool.

Asymmetrical designs never seem to work well on upholstered pieces – they make a chair or footstool look as though it might fall over!

Long stools can be made more interesting by working a pattern reversed along a central line.

A richly-hued drop-in seat in Florentine stitchery is the perfect partner for an antique chair. Gently curving patterns echo the lines of the chair.

Chairs with an upholstered back panel can have the seat pattern adapted to the long narrow shape. Pairs or sets of chairs can either be stitched in the same pattern, changing the order of the colours, or in different patterns, using the same colour scheme. Make sure that the scale and colour balance of the different patterns is the same.

Choosing colours

Try to choose harmonious colour schemes for your upholstered pieces. Avoid loud, jazzy colour combinations which are best kept for cushions. A chair, or a set of dining room chairs, will be more adaptable and easier to live with if the colours are fairly muted and they will probably become family heirlooms.
Check that your chosen colours harmonize with the wood of the furniture and if the needlepoint is intended for a room which is often used in the evenings, look at the colours in the room itself by artificial light.
Do not include too much white or pale colours – they are not as practical as the medium or dark shades.

Chair seat variations

Here are some different patterns obtained by arranging medallions in various ways. Try to balance pale medallions with darker ones and remember that a filling pattern can look quite different in new colours or when inverted.
1 Mix your medallions for a random, patchwork-like effect.
2 Include a central vertical band of identical medallions.
3 Another symmetrical pattern with the centres in dark brown.

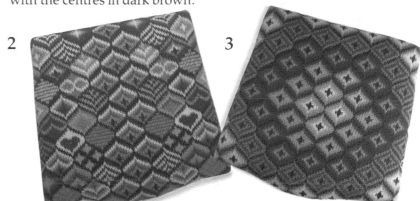

Techniques for drop-in seat covers

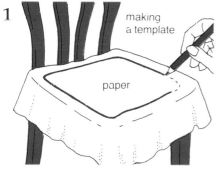

1 making a template
paper

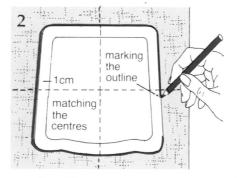

2
1cm
marking the outline
matching the centres

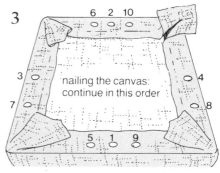

3
6 2 10
3
7
nailing the canvas: continue in this order
5 1 9
4
8

First check that the finished seat when covered will still fit in the chair framework, removing any previous covering if necessary.
If you are making covers for a set of chairs, buy all the canvas and yarn you expect to need at the same time. Keep a record of the amount of yarn used on the first cover so that should any errors or changes of plan occur, more supplies can be purchased in good time.
1 Make a template of the cover from paper or, better still, from a piece of old sheeting. Lay the paper or sheeting over the seat and mark all round where the wooden part of the seat begins. Add 1cm/½in extra

all round and cut out the pattern.
2 Lay the pattern on a piece of canvas which has at least 5cm/2in extra all round the template. Mark the outline with a pencil or waterproof marker. Do *not* cut it out.
Mount the canvas on a frame if you have one – but with these straight stitches this is not essential. Begin in the centre of the canvas and work the first pattern rows horizontally to establish the design. Begin each subsequent row at alternate ends – first work from left to right, then from right to left. This gives an even amount of yarn on the back, helping it to wear well.

The edges of the stitches do not need to be particularly straight – they'll be turned under on the finished seat.
Block and set your finished needlepoint (see page 23).
Upholstering the seat Unless you are confident, it is probably best to have the finished needlepoint mounted professionally. If you wish to do it yourself, make sure that the design is centred on the seat and the canvas is stretched evenly round to the underside.
3 Nail down all round on the underside working from the centre of each edge and alternately from front to back and side to side.

Medallion patterns for a dining chair

The dining chair and seats shown in the picture are part of a set – each one unique. They harmonize well because the medallion outlines are identical on each one and worked in the same rich shade of brown. The same colours – five shades of coral, off-white and two browns – are used throughout in different combinations.

The instructions given here are for the V-shaped seat design which is formed by working different filling patterns in diagonal lines which come to a point at the centre front of the seat. Medallion patterns one to six (opposite) are used for this design – number one in three different colourways.

Use the other medallion patterns to develop your own seat designs. Once you have stitched the basic medallion outlines, have fun mixing and matching the filling patterns in random designs or regular geometric patterns. For examples of both see the Design Extra on the previous page.

You will need
For one chair seat:
1×25g/1oz hank each Appleton's crewel wool in off-white (992), flesh 5 (705), coral 1 (861), coral 2 (862), coral 3 (863), coral 4 (864), chocolate 2 (182)
2×25g/1oz hanks in chocolate 5 (185)
Mono canvas (ecru) 14-gauge
Tapestry needle size 20

Linking the medallions

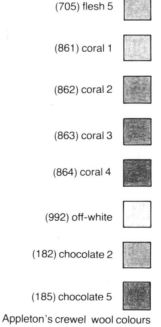

Making the seat
Make a template for the chair seat and mark the area to be worked on the canvas. Mark centre of area. Make a sketch as a reminder to yourself which patterns you intend to place in what order. A scheme is given for the actual design of the V-shaped seat design.

The design motif is formed from a simple curve and peak pattern in mirror image. Stitch the framework of interlocking medallions first, then work one complete chevron of filling patterns to establish the design.

Work the subsequent chevrons starting at the centre out towards each edge. Block and set your finished needlepoint.

Chart for V-shaped seat design

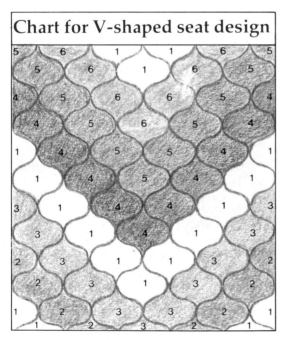

(705) flesh 5		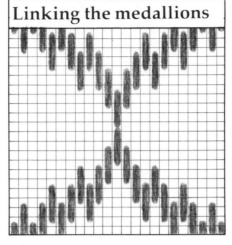

(705) flesh 5

(861) coral 1

(862) coral 2

(863) coral 3

(864) coral 4

(992) off-white

(182) chocolate 2

(185) chocolate 5

Appleton's crewel wool colours

1

flesh 5, off-white, chocolate 2, chocolate 5

5

coral 3, off-white, chocolate 2, chocolate 5

9

coral 1, coral 2, coral 3, chocolate 5

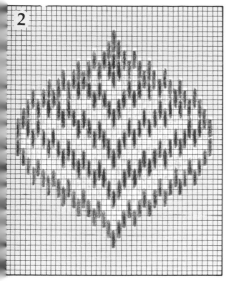

2

coral 4, off-white, chocolate 5

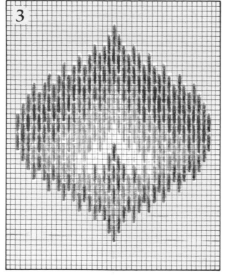

3

coral 1, coral 3, coral 4, off-white,
chocolate 2, chocolate 5

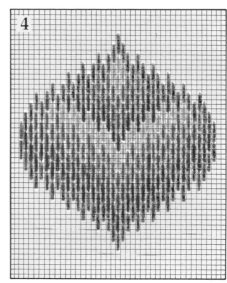

4

coral 1, coral 2, coral 3, coral 4,
chocolate 5

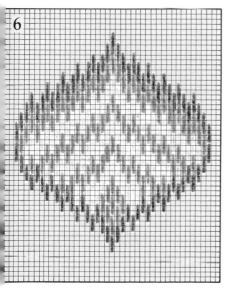

6

flesh 5, off-white, chocolate 5

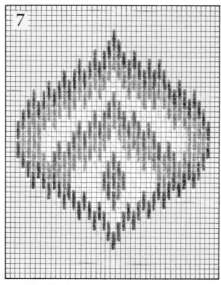

7

coral 2, off-white, chocolate 2,
chocolate 5

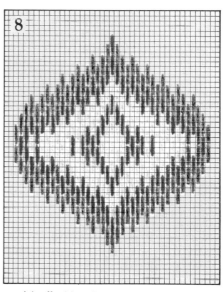

8

coral 4, off-white, chocolate 5

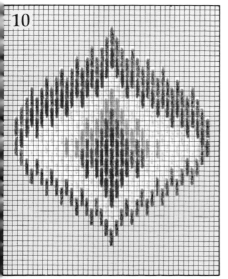

10

coral 1, coral 3, coral 4, off-white,
chocolate 5

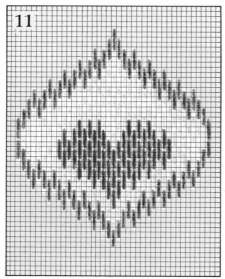

11

coral 4, off-white, chocolate 5

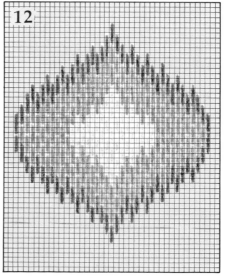

12

coral 1, off-white, chocolate 2,
chocolate 5

83

CHAPTER 16

Fun with plastic canvas

*The ideal medium for exciting three-dimensional needle-
point projects – and perfect for making gifts –
plastic canvas is so easy to work on that children enjoy
using it. Start them off with one of these
pretty items: boxes, baskets or a simple flat key-ring tag*

Plastic canvas is becoming widely available in 7- and 10-gauge sizes. It comes in panels measuring 26.5cm×34.5cm/10½in×13½in. You can also obtain small ready-formed circles, hexagons, diamonds and squares. As it is rigid you do not need to work on a frame, nor block and set the canvas. It cannot fray so it can be cut to the exact thread count required. Accurate counting is essential, however, and miscounting even one thread can waste a whole panel. These instructions show you how to mark planned cutting lines and, after working the needlepoint, how to cut and assemble the individual pieces. The outer edges of the canvas panels are smooth so use these as often as possible as the edges of worked pieces – this makes joining easier. On cut edges, take a pair of sharp scissors and trim off all the 'nubs' carefully to make a smooth finished edge.

Stitching techniques

Although you're not working on a frame, use a 'stabbing stitch' technique rather than working a whole stitch at once. Many types of stitch can be used as long as the coverage is good but try to work all the stitches on one project in the same direction. To join two pieces of canvas, or to cover single edges, use overcast stitch or braided cross stitch.

Below: Versatile plastic canvas can be used to make containers of all kinds.

Overcast stitch

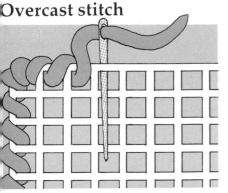

This is a binding stitch worked by simply passing the needle over and over the edge(s) of the canvas, covering one or two of the outside horizontal threads. At corners, it is a good idea to go through the same hole up to three times to obtain good coverage.

Braided cross stitch

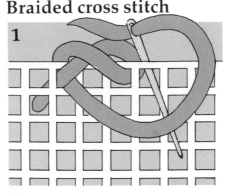

1

2

This stitch gives a pretty plaited effect to edges and corner joins.
1 Bring the needle through from back to front in the first hole, go over the edge to the back and come through two holes away (leaving one free hole).
Go over to the back again and come

through the first hole once more. Go over to the back and come through in the fourth hole, then over and through in the second hole.
2 Repeat step 1 using the fifth and third holes, sixth and fourth holes and so on.

Pretty projects for unusual gifts

Use 7-gauge canvas for all the projects shown in this chapter. Thread the needle with five strands of crewel wool for the tent stitch, overcast stitch and braided cross stitch and eight for all-over stitches. The canvas layout overleaf shows you how to cut three key-ring tags, the red and white basket and the side of the soap basket from the same panel of canvas.
Before beginning to stitch any of the projects, mark cutting lines with tacking in a contrasting yarn as shown on the chart.

Initialled key-ring tags

How about beginning with these flat items – durable initialled tags for key-rings. They are fun to make and can be personalized using the simple alphabet on page 62.

You will need

1 small skein Appletons crewel wool in each of 3 colours
Tapestry needle size 16
Small felt square for backing
Small metal ring (for key-ring)

Making the tag

Count the number of stitches in the width of your chosen letter chart – the tag width may vary depending on the shape of the letter – for instance, the A tag in the picture is one thread wider than the P tag. Mark the tag outline as shown on chart with tacking. Stitch the letter

using continental tent stitch, then fill in with the other colours, working outwards.
Now cut along tacked cutting lines, cutting a hole in the tab part and trimming protruding nubs to make a smooth edge. Bind the cut edges with overcast stitch in the border colour.
Make sure all ends of thread are neatly finished off and trimmed. Glue felt backing in place and add the small metal ring.

Tissue box and soap basket

You'll need two panels of canvas to make these pretty presents but as the chart shows, you'll be left with some offcuts for making any other items. This cover fits a square tissue box, but you could plan one to fit any size of box.

You will need

2 panels 7-gauge plastic canvas
1 circle, diameter 11cm/4½in
2 hanks each Appletons crewel wool in White (991), Bright Rose Pink 3 and 5 (943) and (945)
Tapestry needle size 16

Making the tissue box

First mark the cutting lines with tacking. The stitched design does not share any holes with the tacking. Remember there is no base to the box cover so you only need to stitch one box top – use continental

tent stitch for this and follow the colour key.
Work two large side panels and two small ones in the basket-effect stitch. The centre panels with hearts or butterflies are in tent stitch.
Now cut out the five pieces carefully along tacked lines. Trim off nubs of canvas.
Make up the box using the darker pink yarn. First overcast stitch round square opening in top, then join all four sides together with braided cross stitch (make sure the two larger sides are opposite). This forms the outside of the box. Now join the top to the sides, matching each seam hole for hole, using braided cross stitch.
Finally, overcast the lower edge of the box, covering two horizontal canvas threads.

initialled
key-ring
tag

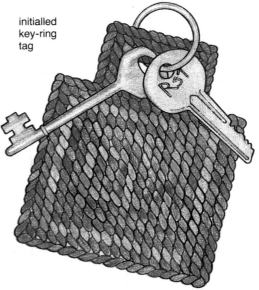

Stitch guide for soap basket base

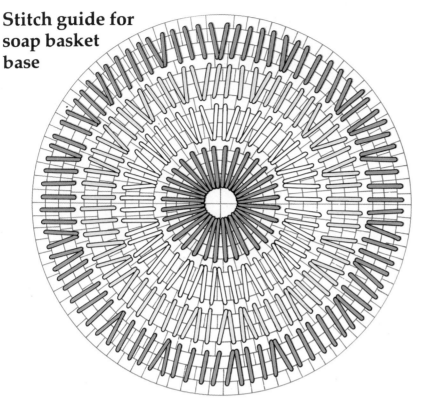

Making the soap basket

Take the plastic canvas circle and work as shown in the diagram – the centre circle stitches spanning four threads and the other three rings spanning three.

Stitch the side panel from the large chart using continental tent stitch. Trim canvas nubs along top edge and join short ends with overcast stitch in white (except for one pink stitch where the hearts touch).

Work pink braided cross stitch round the top edge, and repeat to join base to side panel, matching holes carefully.

Line with a small lace doily, or make a lining using a circle and strip cut from pink felt.

Small gift basket

This little basket is easy to make and is such a pretty receptacle for sweets, soap, dried flowers, a sewing kit, cotton wool balls – anything you like. Of course you can include names and initials in the side panels if you wish.

Stitch guide for remaining pieces

- -	cutting lines
	bright rose pink 5 (945)
	bright rose pink 3 (943)
	white (991)
	bright china blue 7 (747)
	scarlet 1a (501a)

box top

box sides

You will need

1 panel 7-gauge plastic canvas
3 small skeins each Appletons
crewel wool in White (991) and
Scarlet 1a (501a)
Tapestry needle size 16

Making the gift basket

Work the two long sides and the
handle in one piece as shown on the
chart. The white stitches span five
threads, the red stitches one. On
the handle, work only the central
white stitches. Now work the base
of the basket with red for the long
stitches and white for the short.
Work the two ends. Cut the four
pieces out carefully and trim nubs.
Make up using red yarn. Join the
four sides with braided cross stitch,
overcast over two threads round the
top of the basket and on either side
of the handle. Join base to sides
with braided cross stitch.

*Right: This professional-looking basket
is perfect for holding small gifts.*

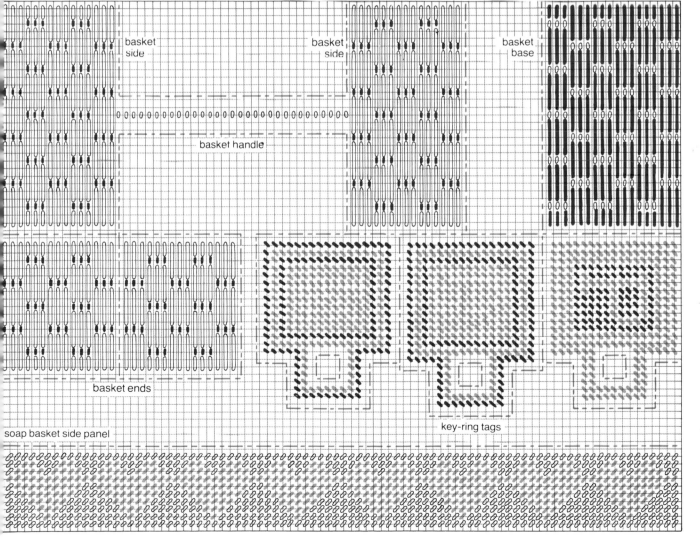

CHAPTER 17

Three-dimensional projects

With careful planning, it's quite simple to stitch an accurate representation of any house you like on canvas. Work it as a picture or make it three-dimensional for the ultimate doorstop! This chapter contains basic know-how, the next covers stitching and making up.

The simple, geometric lines of a house make an ideal project for canvaswork, and the effect of roof slates, bricks, windows and doors can be very well represented using different stitches and threads.

There are two approaches to designing a stitched house – you can either work a flat picture *or* work all four elevations of the house, together with the roof as a three-dimensional piece that could become a doorstop, a large paper weight, or just a unique ornament.

If you choose to make a picture, a front or back view of the house, straight on, works best, because perspective is difficult to represent on canvas.

Left: A house can be fun to stitch and makes an unusual doorstop.

Checklist

1 What canvas do you wish to use? This depends largely on the finished size required and the amount of detail. For a fairly small piece showing a large house with good surface interest such as brickwork and mullioned windows for instance, use a fine-gauge canvas. A plainer (stucco or plastered) exterior with picture windows would be better stitched on a coarser canvas.

2 What colour canvas? This is a personal choice to a certain degree but if the main house walls are white or a pale shade, white canvas is easier to cover, likewise a deep colour house will work up better on ecru or brown canvas.

3 What are the house's dimensions? Check the relative height and width of the house from your photograph or drawing. Do they give you a tall

Three-dimensional, free-standing projects work well if the house is fairly compact. When stitched and made up, these pieces can be filled with wood or foam blocks, cut to fit. Bear in mind, though, that features like low-built back extensions could be tricky to fill.

End (side) walls of houses are often rather ugly – they may have frosted bathroom windows or untidy plumbing, and terraced houses don't have side walls at all.

To solve these problems, work both end walls in an attractive brick pattern to link the front and back. Or use one of the ends to personalize the piece with a stitched 'family tree' showing its occupants.

Preparation

All you need to work from is a straight-on photograph of the view you wish to stitch. An ordinary snap is adequate but a slightly enlarged print is better. If available, a good alternative is an architect's elevation, which is drawn to scale.

If you don't have a colour photograph to go by, make notes on the actual colours. The house will be more fun to stitch if you can include any bushes, plants or trees that grow close to it, so try to take the photograph in summer when the garden is looking at its best.

It is very important to look really hard at the house to assess the scale and relationship of doors to windows, depth of roof to overall height, etc, before drawing the design on the canvas. To do this, take a ruler and notepad and ask yourself ten simple questions (see below).

Choosing materials

Canvas See checklist questions 1 and 2 – the guiding factors being what you are most happy to work on and the quality of detail you wish to represent on the house.

Yarn It is unlikely that this kind of piece will need to be hard-wearing but you will probably be looking for maximum texture and surface interest. Crewel and Persian yarn, stranded and pearl cotton or crochet cotton are all excellent, but anything which appeals to you in knitting or weaving yarns, with regard to colour and texture, is worth experimenting with.

Any kind of thread or yarn can be couched (caught in place with small stitches) on to the canvas surface to add interest and depth to the design. Try this with rug thrums, linen weaving thread, chenille, fluffy mohair or nubbly knitting yarns.

For regular stitching through the canvas, choose a smooth thread and one which is not too thick for the canvas, or it may wear thin before a needleful is finished.

Bushes, plants and flowers

It is only satisfactory to work these in a solid stitch directly on the bare canvas if they are very bushy. Usually it is better to stitch the fabric of the house then use surface embroidery stitches like chain stitch, split stitch, and French knots to add climbing plants to the walls of the house. This is particularly effective on free-standing houses.

To stitch a larger area of garden when working a picture, choose several different shades for foliage and use the darker ones at the back for depth, paler shades towards the front. Pick a small, repeating stitch for small areas and use larger, individual stitches such as triple cross stitch or eyelet to represent single blooms.

Leaf stitch is ideal for leaves and trees, and various other stitches may appeal to you as suitable for plants and gardens. If you don't manage to include them all in the picture, how about using the extra ones in a sampler border round the outside?

or flat finished shape? Is this what you want or do you wish to adjust the shape by adding trees and bushes to the side of the house or grass, paths and hedges to the front, lengthening the foreground? (This applies mainly to flat pictures.)

4 What size do you want the final piece of needlepoint to be? Having decided roughly, work out the relationship between the dimensions in the photograph/plan and the projected finished piece. This will help you both to draw up the design and choose materials.

5 What is the proportion of the roof to the frontage? Many houses, Alpine chalets and thatched cottages for example, depend on their deep roofs for much of their character, so remember this when planning the design.

6 Where is the front door, what is its scale, is there any detail? Again, the 'identity' of a house can depend on its front door. Does it line up with other features such as windows beside or above it?

If the front door has a porch, keep this face-on and flat when stitching a picture. For a free-standing house, it's possible to add the porch as it actually is.

7 Where are the windows? For an accurate representation, look carefully at the arrangement of windows on the house and see if they all align. Are there the same number of panes in each window? Are the panes square or rectangular? If the house has a later extension, or French windows, narrow metal window frames may have been used which are not so wide as those on the rest of the house.

8 Is there any surface decoration that will affect the thread count? As the design must be worked out accurately on the canvas before you begin stitching, take account of any features such as bricks or shutters which require a particular number of canvas threads to be fitted in. If you're using a stitch such as cushion stitch, remember to allow for its thread count, too.

9 Any bushes or climbing plants? Any flowers or foliage you wish to include is best worked as surface embroidery on the stitched house. In this case, choose tent stitch for the walls.

10 Any other detail you wish to add? Besides using artistic licence with the size of bushes (see above), you may wish to add other details such as window boxes, a garden gate, or a different door.

Above: An interesting textural picture derived from Anne Hathaway's cottage (inset). Letting the heavy, thatched roof fill the picture to the top of the frame reinforces its quaint character.

Needlepoint houses

The instructions which follow apply equally to a two dimensonal house picture or three dimensional model.

Planning the design

Whether your photograph is an angle shot, or not, make a straight-on sketch/diagram of the front of the house, as accurately as possible. Mark on it the dimensions you have already taken from the photograph. For three-dimensional houses, make a straight-on sketch of one of the sides as well.

Points to watch

The main exterior features to be fitted in on the chalet shown later in this chapter are the windows, shutters and balconies. Walls and roof can be stitched as all-over effects, adaptable to the rest of the design. Notice that the windows and shutters line up on both storeys, both balconies are the same depth, and the roof overhang is equal all round.

14-gauge canvas was chosen for the chalet piece but study your answers to the checklist given on pages 88–89 to establish what is best for your intended design. The relative dimensions for the finished piece are based on the desired height. For instance, if the height of the building is to be five times its photograph height, multiply all the dimensions by five to keep the house to scale.

Modifying the design

It is sometimes a good idea to use 'artist's licence' and modify the design to make it simpler to stitch. For instance, the actual chalet on which this chapter's project is based (see page 94) is a very deep building with jutting balconies towards the back. It was decided to include only one set of windows on each side, foreshortening the side walls, and to work the chalet as a regular rectangle, with the front and back identical and the two sides identical.

The front and one side wall are worked as one piece, likewise the back and one side wall. The roof is worked in one piece.

To provide interest and attractive detail, window boxes, flowers,

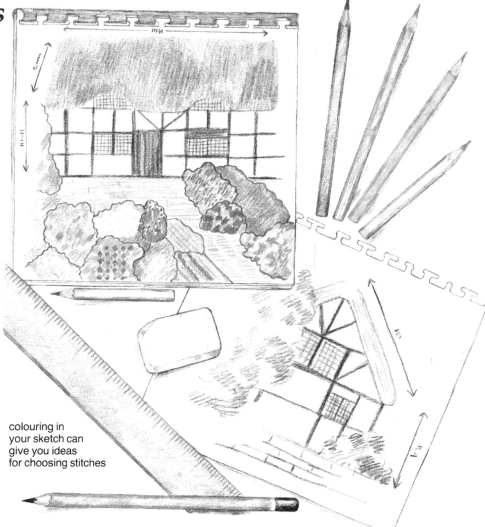

colouring in your sketch can give you ideas for choosing stitches

stacked logs and a bank of snow are added to the design. Sketch these in your first drawing to see the effect. Although the roof is snow-covered, work it in a more interesting mixture of grey and brown, rather than stark white. Scallop satin stitch with Rhodes stitch timber ends makes the roof more attractive.

Transferring design to canvas

Working horizontally The desired width for the chalet was about 25cm/10in, so on 14-gauge canvas, this gave a count of 140 threads. Increasing this slightly to 150 gave 7 threads for each window pane and inside shutter and 2 for each window frame and shutter border, plus an equal amount of plain wall at each end (14 threads).

Working vertically Notice that the roof space is one of the main features and takes up almost one quarter of the total height.

The window panes are shorter than their width and so should span 5

threads or less (width is 7). The horizontal glazing bars are narrower than the main frames, so must be one thread.

Make balconies slightly deeper than windows and plan for a bigger stitch to help the illusion of relief. The desired height gives a thread count of about 175. Allowing 40 for the roof space, you arrive at 24 for balconies, including handrail, 21 for windows, timber cladding under balcony at 16, basement at 30, giving the required window pane count of 5. Calculate for the side and back walls in the same way.

Marking the design Mark all these calculations on a second diagram. Cut and bind the piece of canvas and mark the centre. Mark all the design lines for the front and side walls on the canvas with a pencil, counting threads carefully. Mark the corner of the house. Remember your marks should run along lines of *holes* as this is where stitch ends will fall.

Adding perspective

The photograph of a house is bound to contain areas of shadow which give definition and perspective to it. To portray these realistically on flat or three-dimensional pieces, mix in one or two strands of grey or a slightly darker shade thread than the main colour you are using.
Not all houses are flat-fronted.

Some have projecting areas and extensions, so use scale as well as the shadow techniques to help define them. Consider using a stitch with a smaller thread count for the walls and roof of the recessed part and a larger stitch effect for the forward part (see the two sizes of brick pattern shown opposite).

Roofs, walls and window

Have fun experimenting with colours and stitches to obtain the best effect for the house you are stitching. Spend a little time trying them out on a piece of spare canvas before actually working the house. Here are some commonly-found roof, wall and window effects to start you off. Save up yarn oddments – they could be useful for a house feature.

Roofs

1 and 2 show two different scales of red-tiled roof. Both use double brick stitch, worked horizontally in mixed brick red and brown yarn.
3 and 4 show two variations of grey slate roofs, using straight and sloping gobelin stitch.
Backstitch in a darker thread gives added definition where separate tiles stand out.
5 and 6 show two thatched roof effects – 5 has one end of the couched flecked weaving yarn taken through to the back of the canvas, the other trimmed. 6 shows you the effect of couching a bouclé yarn, both ends are trimmed.

Special effects stitches for house stitchery

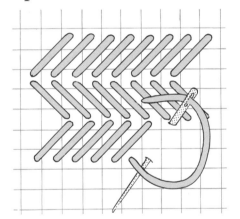

1

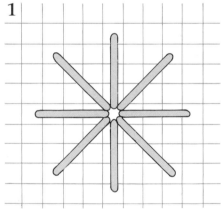

2

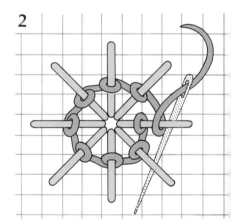

Horizontal knitting stitch
This is a good stitch for surface interest and gives a zigzag effect, used on the chalet shutters.
Knitting stitch can also be worked vertically.
Work diagonal stitches spanning two threads in each direction, then work the next row in the opposite direction, but so that the stitches share holes with the first row.

Whipped spider's web stitch
This is fun to do and useful for details like flowers. It is used in the chalet design for the logs.
1 First set up the framework of straight stitches, converging in the same hole to form a star-shape as shown. Work the stitches in the basic cross over three or four threads, depending on the size you want.

2 Bring the needle up close to the centre of the star-shape and whip it, making sure the needle does not pierce the canvas.
To do this, pass the needle forward under two 'spokes', and back over one, working outwards until all the spokes are covered.

Walls

7 and 8 show the pretty effect of traditional red brick in two scales. The sloping gobelin stitch 'bricks' are surrounded by tent stitch 'mortar'.

Windows

9 and 10 Sloping gobelin stitch used again – here in two different shades of grey to enliven window panes on a white-framed window.

For a diamond-paned leaded window, Hungarian stitch is ideal. Diagonal rows of backstitch in black add the lines of leading.

Other stitches that might well be useful are square mosaic and double brick stitches.

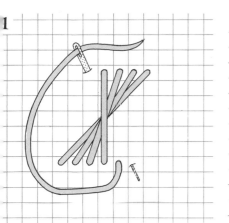

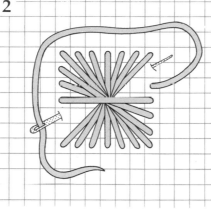

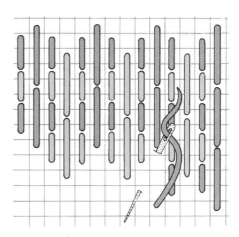

Rhodes stitch

This spectacular stitch forms a large padded square. Work it in single squares or as an all-over filling. The square can cover any number of threads as long as the same basic method is used.

Begin at one of the corners of the square and make a diagonal stitch to the opposite corner.

Bring the needle up in the next hole, going round the edge of the square anti-clockwise, and re-insert it opposite in the hole next to the one where it last went in. A square over six threads is shown here.

2 Continue round the edge until the whole square is filled. If desired, you can add a small upright stitch in the centre to 'tie' all the threads in place.

Hungarian stitch

This is ideal for diamond-paned windows and could come in handy for roofs or gardens.

Working horizontally to form diamonds, make upright stitches over two, four and two threads, leaving two vertical threads free between each diamond.

On the next row, make the long stitches between the previous diamonds. The short stitches should share holes with the previous row.

93

Stitching and decorating the chalet

It is difficult to talk specifically about amounts of canvas and thread you need as these are so variable. For a three-dimensional project like this, (28cm/11in tall, 24cm/9½in wide and 13cm/5in deep), you'll need about two large hanks (25g) of crewel wool in each of nine colours (including, in this case, four different browns and three different greys) plus three or four shades of stranded or pearl cotton for flowers, curtains and highlights.

It is always a good idea to strip down stranded cotton before use as this helps the threads to lie smoothly over the canvas.

Working the walls

Work the house front plus one side first, then the back plus one side. As when you are planning the design, try to establish features like windows and shutters on the canvas first. Work window frames and shutter outlines, using the neat cornering of straight gobelin stitch on both.

Now fill in these areas with the chosen stitch. Horizontal knitting stitch makes the red shutters here look very attractive.

Balconies are another feature to fit in early on. Padded satin stitch makes handrails stand out – lay a double thickness of yarn along the stitching line first of all.

The eight window boxes filled with flowers are fun to include – work the boxes in cushion stitch.

Most of the balcony bars are in straight gobelin stitch in mottled brown yarns; the bars directly above window boxes are worked in tent stitch as the flowers are embroidered later on top.

Timber cladding Before filling in the main body of timber cladding, ensure that you have stitched all irregularities such as shadows and beams.

Encroaching gobelin is a good choice for effects like painted clapboard and natural timber cladding. Try to make the surface as interesting as possible with colour shading, beginning with the two darkest tones in the darkest area, (probably beneath the roof overhang) gradually changing to the lighter shades.

Lower storey area The basement floor of the chalet has stone walls with stone piers supporting the

Below: A three-dimensional Alpine chalet makes an attractive ornament and may bring back holiday memories.

weight of the balcony above. One of them falls at the corner of the house and appears on both front and side walls, so is double the width of the other two on the canvas.

Double brick stitch in mottled grey and white makes effective stone piers; a darker combination is used for the stonework of the walls.

The only other feature to be fitted in is a door (horizontal straight gobelin stitch for contrast).

Work the background areas, where you intend having surface embroidery, in tent stitch, (in this case, the pile of logs on the front wall of the chalet).

Leave the area for the bank of snow unworked – the French knots used for the snow can be worked so densely that there is no need to stitch the canvas underneath as it will not show through.

Surface embroidery

Now add the pile of logs using mixed browns and whipped spider's web stitches placed at random.

Finally, fill the window boxes with pretty flowers using detached chain stitches for green leaves and French knots for the flowers themselves. Work an identical piece for the back and other side wall of the chalet.

Working the roof

For the chalet roof, work a simple rectangle of needlepoint. The width should be the measurement of the side wall, plus back and front overhang allowance (about 1cm/½in) and the length should be the length of both upper sloping chalet front walls plus overhang allowance for both sides. Mark the edges of the roof on the canvas, as well as the centre fold.

To make an interesting feature, work timber ends in a row in chunky Rhodes stitch on either side of the centre top of the roof.

Apart from any foldlines which are worked in straight gobelin stitch, work the main roof area in an attractive scallop pattern satin stitch using a mixture of grey and brown threads. Work compensation stitches of different lengths to make the front, back and side edges straight.

At the front and back edges of the roof overhang, along marked lines, leave two free threads of canvas and fill the underneath portion with the same satin stitch. Now fold the canvas back on itself along unworked threads and cover these with a row of straight gobelin stitch to make a firm fold.

Making up the finished work

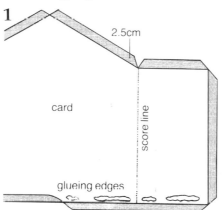

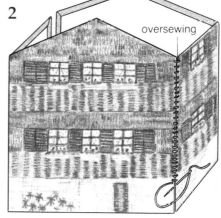

If you've made the chalet or other house as a flat picture, stretch the canvas and mount it on a panel of hardboard cut to fit (see page 27). Do not cover the piece with glass – use a deeply-recessed frame to protect it.

Three-dimensional projects

Here is the method for making up a square or rectangular house, like the chalet, which is made up in two pieces, plus the roof.

1 Cut two pieces of firm card to the exact size and shape of the front plus side and back plus side. With a craft knife, score the card down the two corners of the house. Trim canvas around needlepoint to 2.5cm/1in and lay over pieces of card. Turn spare canvas to the underside and glue firmly in place. Mount the roof piece in exactly the same way, scoring the card along the roof centre.

2 Using matching wool, oversew the two wall pieces together along the two opposite corners.

The filling depends on the intended use. For a sturdy doorstop, fill the house with a standard brick bonded to blocks of wood cut to form a base for the house.

Glue wood in place.

For a lightweight, purely ornamental piece, use a block of firm foam cut to the exact shape, or thick polystyrene tiles glued together and cut to shape.

Place the bent roof in position and catch it in place at intervals along upper edges of house walls.

Index